Initiation of the Flame

Laura Anne

Reviews of *Initiation of the Flame*

"When I started working with Laura as her book coach, I knew she was about to write a wonderful book, but she has completely blown me away with what she has created. Initiation of the Flame is not just another spiritual or self-help book. This is a book that bypasses your mind to speak directly to the soul, and the messages it contains stay with you long after you've finished reading it. Indeed, you can feel its power and magic working through you, shifting and transforming you from within. What Laura has written is a book that comes directly from her soul to yours. I am deeply humbled and honoured to have had the chance to support her in birthing this magic into the world."

~ Katie Oman- Editor and book coach. https://www.katieoman.co.uk/write-your-magic

"If you're looking for a wake-up call to live your best life, then this is the book for you. I was set alight, ignited and enlightened by 'Initiation of the Flame'. Laura Anne, lets us into her own life experiences, as well as helping us to deal with making the best of our own history, present and future! If you don't have this book, you're missing out. If

you're lacking tools, then this is where you'll find them! Laura Anne, your book blew me away! You had me up all night last night finishing it and I've woken up wanting to read it all over again. When you write it as if you are speaking directly to me. Your connection will reach so far, you've found a way to give people the tools they need to live their best life."

~ Claire Petulengro- Renowned astrologer, celebrity clairvoyant, author, and dear friend.

"A brave and honest depiction of Laura Anne in all her many forms: daughter, partner, mother, empath, victim, survivor, teacher of empowerment but, ultimately, 'Happiness Maker.' She shares stories of how the brutal lessons in her life taught her how to overcome adversity, fight back and achieve her dreams.

A spiritual awakening revealed Laura's many talents, including her gift of being intuitive, enabling her to go on to help many people in need as well as taking her on a journey of self-discovery. Women all over the world will be able to identify with Laura's own fears, worries and vulnerabilities. This is not a preachy self-help book but an insightful guide to encourage us to come to terms with our own difficulties and differences. Laura gives us the tools in the form of helpful solutions, prompts and epilogues at the end of each chapter.

Laura's strong but kind personality runs through the whole of the book with her 'don't accept' but 'question' attitude and messages of embracing who we are and connecting with our flow of energy.

Laura Anne is a shining light. Her book is not only informative and inspiring but truly life changing."

~Jacquie Tyler- Book critic, writer for Lengro Magazine, entrepreneur, and inspiring woman.

"This book will resonate with so many. Deeply relatable whilst hugely magical, Laura navigates some difficult topics with grace without losing the impact of the lessons learned. Best of all, this is not "just" one woman's story, but holds wider truths and lessons throughout. It is as much a guidebook as it is an autobiography!"

~ Alex Coward- Business mentor & strategist - *"Success Without Sacrifice."*

- With special thanks to Marie-Claire Ashcroft - The Professional Rebel, front cover (original) image photographer.

Dedication

This book is dedicated to all the women - Mothers, Daughters, Grandmothers, Sisters, Aunties, Wives, Girlfriends and Friends who have in some form experienced adversity, hurt, trauma, judgement, shame, discouragement, and pain. Any form of negativity that has kept Her bound from discovering, embracing, becoming and embodying Her true self. But it is also dedicated to those of you who despite that, have blossomed and thrived. Wherever you are in your own story, I want to celebrate you, and remind you that regardless of circumstance, you are a powerhouse, a queen, a goddess, an incredible being, and you are so worthy of living the life you've dreamed of!

I'd love to give a special mention to the women in my own life too, the ones who have filled me with love, inspiration and been alongside me on my own journey of self-discovery and growth. These are my daughter Imogen Rose; my mum – Sue; my Grandma Linda; my sister Caroline; my art studio partner and dear friend Lex; and my best friend in the whole world, (Possum) Beth. There have also been many other special women that have impacted my life in such incredible ways, you know who you are. That love, and gratitude extends to you all, my mentors, my friends, and also those of you who have trusted me to be part of your own journeys. I'm incredibly proud and so blessed to witness you bloom into the woman you are today.

A notable mention goes to Katie Oman, for supporting me on my writing journey during the creation of this book. For keeping me accountable, for holding space and listening to me. For also giving me reality checks when I needed them, for being an all-round beautiful soul, and for helping me birth this book into the world.

I also want to give special thanks to the man who has stuck with me all this time and sees me for who I truly am. Who still supports, motivates and loves me unconditionally, even through my weird, wonderful and dark times. Marc, I love you!

And perhaps not the done way, but here I also give thanks to me! A big ol' *"F yes! You go girl!"*. For taking the leap, to trust in myself, for embarking on a journey of self-discovery, growth and doing the inner and outer work. My journey will never be complete; I will never be fully healed. I will never know everything; however, I am so looking forward to growing my knowledge, life, body and energy experiences, conscious connection and to continue experiencing the beautiful world around me! I've got this far, I can't stop now! I'm also excited to embark on the journey of writing this book, as not only am I sharing my story with the intent to inspire, but the writing of this book will be a deep healing journey in itself. I'm curious to see what moves through and the experiences I encounter along the way.

Beautiful woman, dearest reader - I also dedicate this book to all of you. In the hope that it serves as a pillar of light and strength, to give you the support, wisdom, inspiration and insight that I really needed at one point, but never had. That you may feel seen, understood and held in a way that feels safe. This is the book I wish I had, and now it is my gift to you!

To my "two babies" - Levi John James and Imogen Rose.

I hope this book leaves you a legacy of love and abundance.

You are my joy and my inspiration. To see you both thrive is the greatest gift of all.

Contents

Reviews of Initiation of the Flame	1
Dedication	4
Introduction	9
Not Quite the Beginning	14
Pretty Little People Pleaser	19
A Stealing of Innocence	26
The Body That Wasn't Mine	34
You Get to Be	44
The 'A' Hole	47
Spiked	56
Special Connections	66
Not Everybody Is Your Friend, But They Are a Lesson!	74
Selfishness Is a Must	83
The Squeeze & The In-Between	94
I Didn't Know I Was	103
Stereotypes And Surface Level Spirituality	111
Finding Your Flow	124
You Can Lead a Horse to Water, But Should You?	136
Deeply Stored Wounds	142
The Women (Ancestral Healing)	154
All Hail the Golden Child	163
Spirit Guides & Higher Power	170
My Sacred Places (Follow the Call)	185
She Who Is Birthed Through Fire	193
Initiation Of the Flame	198
She is Here	204
Epilogue	209

Helpful Link Page	216
Soul Musings	217
Guidance Readings	231

Introduction

How many times have you ever been told no? How many times have you held back or not done something because either someone said you couldn't, or you feel like you couldn't because you worried about how someone else would react, how you may be judged, you worry that it won't work, or that you're not capable?

Maybe you know who you are but have been afraid to unleash Her out into the world truly as She is. Perhaps you're at a point where you don't know…you just don't know who you are, what you want, what you enjoy…. all the things. And that's okay, for now!

This book is here to help you to set ablaze to the mindset of not being enough. To torch the inner fear of being yourself, and to ignite that fire within you that will set your world alight so you can say *"bye-bye"* to all that doesn't fit and say *"hello and welcome"* to the life you've always desired! To come home to Her: your true essence and authentic self.

"But Laura, I'm scared!"

Trust me, so was I, and that is why I'm writing this book. To show you where I came from, what I've been through and who I've become...so far! That's not in any way to gloat and be like *"look at me!"*, but to show you that, despite the life you've lived up until this point, it's possible to create shifts, to learn, to grow, and to know that you CAN thrive too! Regardless of what you've been through or where you're at now, I want to show you through my own story, that there IS a way forward, upwards and outwards. That you are ultimately in control, even if right now it feels like you're not. We can't control what goes on around us, but we CAN control how we react and move forwards.

As well as my own personal story, this book will entice you through your own journey, with snippets of intuitive guidance and channelled Soul musings (and splashes of profanity!) dotted throughout. I've made it no secret that I've been through various things in my life, but this is the first time I have so openly shared such specific details of my story, my experiences and my emotions. I am sure there will be many reactions to my story, from those who know me personally, and those who have never met me, but the reaction I hope to invoke most is inspiration. Inspiration to be the YOU that you know you are. I don't write to request sympathy or sadness. True, there are parts of my story that are downright awful, but the reason I share them so vividly is for transparency, so you, the reader, know that I come from both a place of honesty and openness. I also want you to know that I'm not some 'spiritually aligned know it all' preaching from an untouched ivory tower.

I know that there are many books out there with the promise of inspiration, transformation and motivation, but this one is mine - my story, my experiences, my and musings, and I thank you for choosing me! For being here, now - in this moment - wherever you are, and dedicating time and space to not only my words, but to you.

This book, for the most part, will be my personal experiences and opinions, and so I implore you to maintain your own values and opinions, and to be discerning. However, even though this book is about my story, I intend it to act as a voice, an advocate, and as recognition for the girls, women and people who have endured tough times, come through similar, and are looking for the strength to be themselves. To finally feel like they can stand in their own power, make decisions for themselves, and show up in fully aligned self-embodiment. To live a life aligned with why you came here in the first place!

In my lifetime, so far, I've experienced a lot. Some great highs, but some incredibly low lows. I'm touching upon them in this book, but not because I want to magnetise pity and sympathy. I'm not sharing my story with the intent of being held gently and told how strong I am. I have been there many times. I know I am strong. I appreciate the encouraging words. But this telling of my story, this version, this perspective, is not from the girl who fell victim too many times, or the one who struggles to speak up and be counted. It is not from the one who would appease just to lead an easy life. Nor is it from the one who was drenched in sadness with the weight that her past bore upon her. This perspective is not from my wounded self, or this would be a completely different and uninspiring book!

This is the perspective of the woman who has survived and has overcome. The one who has learned from her mistakes but is still open to make more and learn from them. The one who sees the world through different eyes. The woman who is keen to learn and grow so she can be the best version of herself. The woman who approaches any challenges or opportunities with a forward-thinking perspective, rather than a wounded victim perspective.

So, if anything, this book, this story, is told with the intention of touching the hearts and minds of those who may see parts of themselves in my story, and be inspired that they CAN! To know that despite circumstance, trauma and any other factors, you are so capable and so worthy. That you are not here to merely survive in a wilderness of fear, trauma, hurt, disbelief. You are here to overcome, to thrive and stand tall, as a pillar for yourself, and your lineage, past, present and future. That you are capable of breaking the chains that have felt like shackles for far too long. Know that you can break free, from past life, ancestral and current life patterns of negativity, and you can truly step into, embody and live the life your Soul came here to lead!

This book is also a keen reminder that spirituality is not all love, light and rainbows. If it seems to be, then you may not be as deep down the 'rabbit hole' as you think! *Initiation of the Flame* is a frank, honest and open book about self-discovery and spirituality. Yes, there are times of light, but also in dark and shadow. Both are equally as valid and needed as the other; the key here is duality! Without it, we cannot know or experience balance, or the contrast needed to be the catalyst for change and motivation. If you are looking for a 'care bear-esque' book on how to be spiritual, this is not it!

Not Quite the Beginning...

  I reached a point in my life where I knew things HAD to change. And when I say 'things', I mean me! I had to change!

But why? What was wrong with me? By this point, life had well and truly chewed me up and spat me out, and I was in no fit mental state to even try and get back up again. I was carrying the heavy burden of childhood trauma (which I was much later diagnosed with having P.T.S.D.) and I had also not long been diagnosed with chronic illness. I was exhausted, in pain, mentally, emotionally and physically, on a cocktail of meds, as well as more meds for the post-natal depression I was trapped within after giving birth to my second child, To add to that my first child was in amongst the lengthy process of an autism diagnosis.

My relationship was also being tested at this point. We were a young family. I had issues with my mental and physical health, we were caring for a new daughter and trying to get our head around how to best support our son's needs. My partner was working hard at his family business, only bringing in a minimal income, while I was bringing in no income at all. Times were really hard for us at that point. I felt vacant, like I couldn't be present in my own body, or in my own life. Feeling like a burden.

I was wiped out on medication most of the time, and when I actually was able to stay awake, I wanted to just sleep, hide out and cry. ALL. THE. TIME!

Even though my partner was super supportive, I still felt isolated. I had no family living near by - the joys of coming from a military background is that everyone is dotted around the country (or overseas). So, I didn't have my parents, siblings or grandparents on my doorstep to chip in and help. His family were nearby, but I already felt like too much of a failure to reach out and cry for the help I so desperately needed. By this point, my social anxiety had gotten so bad that I had isolated myself from most of my friends, in fear they either secretly hated me, would judge me or that I would talk too much, say something stupid and then panic about it for days after I saw them.

The me then was nothing like the me now. In fact, I wasn't very me then at all! And this is why I knew it had to change. I wasn't honouring myself, or my needs, and I certainly wasn't in tune with who I came here to be. I was more like an empty shell, not really living, merely existing from one day to the next. Stuck within a vicious cycle of self-loathing, mental and emotional distress and physical pain.

From that point, it wasn't as if I'd had some magical revelation, and overnight I sparkled and shone into a wise, aligned, healed woman. Ha-ha! If only! It was an up and down journey from there, and even to now. At this point, it wasn't a (conscious) journey of Soul connection and discovery, but of merely becoming aware of the basics - simple basic needs - that I had either forgotten, or just treated as a rare luxury, rather than a necessity, and THAT is why I feel a lot of us lack. Because we feel so much guilt or shame in meeting our basic needs that, when we actually do them, it feels like either a treat, or that in doing so we have to restore the balance and work harder or punish ourselves to make up for it. Check out this list. Decide if, to you right now, they are a luxury, a treat, or a necessity.

- A trip to the supermarket…. with NO kids!

- A soak in a hot bubble bath.

- A bunch of flowers that you bought yourself for yourself.

- 10 minutes to drink a tea or coffee while it's still hot.

- Free time to do housework.

- A brisk walk.

- A healthy, balanced meal.

- Social time with friends.

This may come as a surprise, but they are ALL just basic needs or necessities. They are things that we shouldn't feel "lucky" that we have the opportunity to do. However, in our busy or pressured lives, it has become commonplace that we celebrate these as little wins. Sometimes feeling we have to savour them because they are like gold dust!

But it's here where the work begins. If you can't afford yourself basic needs, then how are you going to be in the mindset to really gift yourself true love and dedication?! To not only gift yourself but others the opportunity to receive the best version of you?

At this point, if you are reading this book, I'm going to assume that you are either in that place right now, or at one point in your life you have been, so you probably have a clear idea of what I'm talking about. The guilt sets in, you're prioritising everybody else, your needs and wants go to the bottom of the pile, and you can't spend time or money on this because it would be better spent on x, y, and z. You can't do "that" because [x] won't approve, or they'll have something to say about it and it's not worth the hassle. You talk yourself out of doing things for yourself. Likely because of the way we have been conditioned and the life stories we have grown to falsely believe which are engrained in our minds. And it takes for us to unlearn all of that, to reach a head space where we can shed the guilt and worry of actually choosing "Me" or putting ourselves first for a change. To then begin to trust ourselves.

What we are drawn to.

How we present ourselves.

What we want to eat, drink, create.

Where we want to go.

Who we want to connect with.

How we spend our time and money.

What and who we give energy to.

All of this shifts and up levels when you trust in you. But getting there can be a journey in itself.

Throughout this book, I will share with you my own journey of self-love and trust, intertwined with a concoction of [self-perceived] failures, traumas and triumphs, which I hope may inspire and elevate you on your own journey.

Pretty Little People Pleaser

I remember my childhood so vividly. That's the way my brain works. I remember everything visually in images, like a movie, replaying in my mind, able to quickly skim back to the chapter my mind is focusing on and metaphorically hit play. And so, this isn't just a re-telling, but in doing so, I'm re-watching, viewing those memories with the mindset and experience I have now. I am able to look back into how I experienced life then, but with these eyes now. As I write this, I'm also curious to know what emotions will move through and how I may react. Will I forgive? Will I be hurt or angered? Will I fall completely in love all over again?

Growing up I was…. complacent. The blonde-haired, blue-eyed girl who would often be found quietly drawing pretty pictures. Of course, I had sass. What young girl doesn't?! But I was mostly the good girl. The girl that did as she was told. The girl who didn't want to draw attention or cause a fuss. The girl who wanted to be quietly acknowledged, but not cast into any form of limelight. I hated the thought of any form of conflict or confrontation. I always felt the need to mediate or keep the peace, not to stir the pot or create any kind of negative attention or response. A total people pleaser.

The fear of being disliked really scared me. But even in trying to remain neutral, or to stay out of people's way, to aim to please, to be polite, and not to ruffle feathers, it seemed I would still receive some sort of negative response from people.

I was either seen as too weird, too quiet, or an over sharer to those who seemed to take an interest in me. More often than not, I was overlooked, but when the focus was on me, for some reason it wasn't usually for positive reasons. I think my Soul came here with a strong sense of naivety, to want to see the good in the world and to be the good in the world. And perhaps that is one of the things I am here to unlearn? No matter how much you try, there are always people that will see you in the wrong way, judge you on a snippet of information or talk about you to others to feed their own egos to deflect from their own shadow selves. They project their wounds onto others and still leave you feeling like you're wrong.

So where did this story really begin?

I was born into a military family with a long history of family members serving in the armed forces. It was just the way of life; I knew no other way. Moving, literally from post to post. Getting used to meeting new people, different homes and different places. I knew no different. Many months would be spent with Dad deployed or away on "exercise". And so, I became very close with my Mum from a young age. We've always shared a special bond, even now.

Despite my age and lack of life experience, I always felt like a little helper, a ray of sunshine, and a tiny confidant to be there when times were tough. To cheer her up, to make her smile, and to be a little bit of happiness when she felt down. (*Perhaps that's the old Soul in me - befriending and supporting those older than me has become quite a penchant of mine.*) I got so used to being there for my Mum. Not that she actually needed me (or maybe she did?) but because we were a team, doing my best to help and doing what I could for her to be happy. I didn't want to ever contribute to making her feel sad in any way.

At age 7, my parents split up. Although I didn't realise it at the time, I was a big emotional support for my Mum. I would draw her pictures of the fun and happy life we would go on to have, and we would dance together in the kitchen to *"Things Can Only Get Better"*. We really were a team! I loved to see her happy, knowing that was my doing. She worked 3 jobs to support me and my sister at an age younger than I am now. I look back, as a mother of my own two children, truly admiring her strength. For a long time, I was too caught up in my own wounds and life stories, that I failed to see my Mum from this perspective. But now, although we are two very different people, with different opinions, taste and ideas, I really do have a deep appreciation for her because, not only did she do so much to support us when I was younger, but over the years she has triggered me in ways that have opened me up to my own learning and experiences. This includes assessing how I react to others, how I respond and take on board other people's comments and opinions, and ultimately knowing that I can listen to and take on others input while still standing in my own power and making my own decisions. My Mum has been more of an influence than I ever realised, and I really am grateful for her!

I love you, Mum!

(*My Mum later married my now "Dad" who I'll refer to as Dad in this book. As I write this book, they are nearing their 25th wedding anniversary.*)

Anyway, I digress….

At a young age, I embodied this early sense of maturity. Subsequently, I subconsciously developed the want, no, more like the need, to always please. To be the good one, or as my siblings would go on to call me "the Golden Child". (Although being the golden child isn't all it's cracked up to be, but I'll go into that in a later chapter) Not just the need to please my Mum though, but everybody. I'm not saying that was a behaviour developed because of my Mum, but just me, the life path my Soul chose to slip into, my Soul self, stepping into being of service from a very early age. Knowing what she came here to do and be, but at this point it was a very raw version that didn't know her own boundaries or how to self-regulate.

However, growing up, I continued to strive to please. But as I now know - you can't please everybody! I took it so personally. Sometimes even before the chance of interaction, I would pre-empt feeling the fear of getting it wrong. I'd experience that gut wrenching feeling of over analysis, playing in my mind what they would say and how they would react. Would they laugh at me? Would I offend or make them feel uncomfortable? Would I say something that altered their perception of me?

So, to people outside of my close family circle, I was often the quiet, shy one. The one who would do as she was told (or at least try). The one that would go along with other people's plans and ideas, despite having my own great ideas. I was the one who would keep quiet and uncomfortable, rather than speak up and risk making somebody else feel uncomfortable. A girl who was so self-consumed with trying her very best not to make anyone feel a certain way, not to incite anger, sadness, embarrassment, awkwardness, or any form of negativity, yet would sacrifice her own comfort and happiness to achieve that. In turn, experiencing all of those emotions myself, just to prevent others from feeling them.

This was echoed through my friendships; I was usually the submissive one. Often being friends with louder, boisterous, outgoing - often bossy - children. I didn't want to be in charge, I was too afraid to lead and get it wrong. I wanted others to tell me what to do and I'd just play along. Even into my teens and early 20's. I was too scared to take the reins and to be responsible. Which was ironic, seeing as I had already stepped into the role of self-appointed "happiness maker" - which bore a BIG responsibility.

But this complacent, well behaved, good girl, do-not-disturb attitude did me no favours. I developed many toxic relationships, on the foundations of subservience and obedience. I let people get away with upsetting or hurting me without a word spoken on my part. I didn't want to rock the boat and speak up, telling people if I disagreed, or if they had upset me. I'd rather just stay quiet and keep the peace. *"No"* was a word I found difficult to express. Either saying *"Yes"* to please, or barely saying anything at all, becoming a passive by-stander in my own life for years.

This brings me to 9-year-old me. That innocent, people pleasing nature of mine was taken advantage of, in the worst of ways. A story that those closest to be are aware of, but one I have never publicly shared, until now.

*Mini Epilogue: - From the other side looking back on this chapter, there's not a great deal to elaborate on in terms of what was, but from when I wrote the chapter to almost finalising this book, I can look back on this from a more evolved and aware version of myself. I feel sad that I defaulted to the complacent people pleaser, but

with respect to my past and current self, I can make conscious choices now to be me and do my thing. However, that people pleasing version of me is hard wired into my system and even now can still be a difficult habit to break!

A Stealing of Innocence

(Trigger Warning- includes experiences of sexual abuse. Feel free to skip this chapter if you wish to)

A man [I use the term loosely] more than 7 times my age, touching me in the most private of places, violating my innocence, abusing my trust, abusing my body and forcing himself onto me. This wasn't the first time, but it was the last time he would ever touch me.

As we sat together watching TV, his arm around me, I could feel a scratching sensation down below. His hands were in my underwear, but I didn't know what to do. I didn't know it was wrong or what he was trying to do. So, I just sat there and put up with it. Next the kisses, his stale cigar breath forced onto me. Then he got up and disappeared from the room. My relief short lived as I heard him call me from upstairs. I followed…

Strangely, I remember disassociating from what was happening, but remembering all of the details around me. The dressing table with the china doll, the shelves filled with Catherine Cookson books, and the redundant walking aid in the corner of the room that belonged to his late wife. The door to the left, dresser to the right, window behind my head, the feminine frilly bed set, yet I don't really remember his face. Just a blank silhouette with white hair.

The weight of his body still haunts me, the pressure of his tongue trying to be forced inside my mouth while I pursed my lips shut as tight as I could. I struggled to breathe. I was hurting and in panic as he forced himself on me. I remember being asked, *"Do you like it?"*

No! I absolutely did not! But through fear of displeasing…. Pah! Displeasing (?!)…displeasing the very person who was hurting and abusing me…I said nothing. Afraid to say no, scared to say stop, too nervous to say that he was hurting me. Unaware of what was actually happening to me, but knowing deep in my gut that it wasn't right, I still remained in that state of maintaining the peace and not wanting to cause a fuss.

Luckily, the doorbell rang - the window cleaner. Which led him racing downstairs, fastening his trousers in haste to answer the door as if nothing was going on. *(The thought that the cleaner would have been looking through that window into the room blissfully unaware of what took place makes me shudder even more!)* I took that as my opportunity to get away. So, I grabbed the dog, collar and lead and darted out of the back door. Without a coat or warm clothes during a cold November day, I circled the block over and over and over. Shaking with fear, shivering with cold. Waiting to be picked up so I could go home. Afraid to go back in the house with him. As I was walking down the street with the dog, my parents arrived. I let on that I was just out walking the dog but had forgotten to take my coat. But it was that evening I spoke up and told my parents what had happened, not realising the severity of what it was.

That wasn't the first time he had treated me that way, but it was the last! I remember previously staying over and being awoken in the night to my pyjamas pulled down and a strange 'thing' squashed between the back of my thighs, then my hand being forced to hold something behind me that felt horrible. Then the fear. I thought I had wet the bed because all I could feel was this wet 'stuff' on my legs. In embarrassment, I ran to the bathroom, trying to wipe and clean myself, but it felt like it just wouldn't wipe away. The bathroom door was a sliding door with a little hook latch, which meant even though it did lock, it could still be opened by a couple of centimetres. I remember as I cleaned myself in a panic, looking up at his eyes peering through the gap at me. Those eyes in that gap are burnt into my memory, a painful visual of the panic and shame I felt, even though I had no real idea at the time what had happened.

For years, I would look back and be angry that I never said anything to him - not on the sofa, not in the bed, not in the bathroom. Not no, not stop, nothing. Now I don't look back with anger at myself, as I know that none of that was on me. It wasn't my responsibility to prevent or stop it. I look back with anger at the very person who never should have put me in that situation in the first place. He was the one to blame. The one who knew what he was doing but did it anyway.

The 'accusations' were then taken further, but he took the cowards way out with a rope before anything could go to trial, for the evidence was too strong against him. This in turn left me without real closure, which left him without real accountability. And then that was that. The case closed and we barely spoke of it. But for me, I was left with the mental and emotional burden I would carry for years and, at this point in time, still do.

But what he did to me does not define who I am today. I believe that who I have become is more a reflection of my own true strength. Strength that was always there, regardless, but shone through brighter. As an artist, we say that light makes darks appear darker, and darks make lights appear lighter. And so, all that situation did was provide contrast. It did not serve me in any "everything happens for a reason" kind of way. That said, I still feel deep hurt and sadness. I feel ashamed to live in a world where there are beings that find it acceptable. Where innocence can be so cruelly taken away.

From there, it was like it didn't really happen. We just didn't talk about it, not between myself and anyone else anyway, and at the time I really didn't want to anyway. After the police investigation and having to tell it various times, I'd had enough of reliving it. But then, even years after it all, I was too afraid to bring it up, for fear of upsetting anyone or making them feel uncomfortable having to listen to my trauma story. But now I share this story with confidence, knowing that it is MY story. My experience to keep or to share. In my own way. It took me a long time to realise that it IS okay to share my story, and actually, doing so is a form of therapy in itself. Over the years, I've journaled and written loosely on the details of my experience and also in great depth exactly what happened to me. But I have never shared with anyone else, just a private outlet.

I am 1 in 20, but I am not a statistic. And neither are you! We are more than a number on a spreadsheet. We are more than a crime reference number. We are more than a "victim". We are amazing warriors! We each have our own stories, whether we tell them or not. We may bravely carry our battle scars on the inside, or bravely show them on the outside.

We may feel guilt or shame.

We may worry that people will view us differently when they find out.

We may constantly relive things in our mind.

We may be triggered by the smallest things.

We may reach out and get support.

We may be suffering in silence.

We may be overprotective of our own children.

We may have been reckless with our life choices.

We may have done things and really not cared about the consequences.

We may have restricted ourselves from doing things because we were too worried about the consequences.

We may see the world differently to how others do.

We may judge people differently and be more wary and cautious.

We may seem happy all the time.

We may seem miserable all the time.

We may be open about our trauma.

We may not speak about our trauma.

We are real people and we are navigating life, just like everyone else. But we also may have a different viewpoint to others. Never question our why or how. Never make us feel like we are being too much or too little. Never invalidate how we feel. Never tell us how we should or shouldn't feel. Never think that it is okay to doubt somebody's trauma. Never think that it is okay to tell them to "get over it". Never get into a "who had it worse" competition. We have all got to where we are now in our own path. You have not walked their path, equally they have not walked yours. But you are here now. You now have the choice to do amazing things. You have the ability and the opportunity to be whoever the hell you want to be. You can do, be and say whatever you want to. You have the opportunity to be HAPPY! You have the opportunity to be truly YOU!

I am 1 in 20, but I do not let that hold me back! I have faced all of the above, as well as what I've spoken of in this book, and more. But I make decisions FOR me, unapologetically! Not to please someone who doesn't give two shits about me, not really. Not to massage the ego of those who think I am less than them. Not to prove a point to anybody, except myself! I have suffered and my experience and emotions are valid, but I get to prove to ME that I have overcome, and I choose that I GET TO WIN!!!

Take this as your cue to take back you! Take back your life and fill it with what lights you up - what you want to do, be and say, and enjoy it! Revel and bask in the glow of being beautifully you, without fear, regret or doubt. For you are beautiful in so many ways. If you are 1 in 20, 1 in 5, 1 in 3 or 1 in any other number, know that you are so much more than a statistic.

You own your own power and are in control of your own destiny.

Just know that whatever your experience, it is YOUR story, to share as you want to, to know that you do not need permission. Even if other people disagree with you, or recall differently, we each experience life differently and we feel differently. So, just because they say otherwise, that doesn't discount or invalidate how you feel or what you've been through. Equally, regardless of how uncomfortable your story may be for others, rest in the knowing that there are those who may find solace and inspiration in your story. And that is why I tell mine.

Mini Epilogue: - I've lost count of how many times I've re-read this chapter, thinking I should edit, cut out and soften it to make it more palatable. But what happened to me is not palatable, nor are any similar experiences. So, in honour of myself and those who either have shared their story, or are privately bearing theirs, I share mine. Another torch in the darkness, lighting a pathway, a beckon of recognition, a pillar of resonance, hoping that this will contribute to the net of light that will eventually light up the world and create space and opportunity for us. Not only to just feel seen and heard, but to feel safe and secure in being seen and heard too.

The Body That Wasn't Mine

In the years that would follow on from my abuse, I knew that what happened to me was wrong, but I still had no concept of boundaries, emotionally or physically. I had no real understanding of what was and wasn't appropriate, and so I unmeaningly gave up ownership of my own body. Allowing myself to be touched and treated in ways that, I now know, were unacceptable. Letting people see and touch parts of me, whether they were aware or not that they were taking advantage or that they were interacting with an empty shell. A capsule of emptiness, not giving willingly because that was what she wanted, but because she had already relinquished that part of herself. The void was numbing; a platform for disassociation. A space where my own body felt separate from my being.

I remember on swimming trips with school, two of the boys in the year above would corner me in the pool, demanding to see my breasts, or to 'prove' that I had pubic hair. I knew it wasn't right, but I didn't really understand how wrong it actually was. And so, I would do it. Despite me being quite emotionally mature, on reflection, I realise how childlike, oblivious and naive I was for so long.

"Slut!" then became a familiar word.

Despite trying to keep my head down, blend in and be liked without fuss in high school, again, as I neared my last year, I trusted the wrong people, and this was reflected in this somewhat promiscuous reputation that was created of me. Despite the fact that I hadn't actually lost my virginity until I was almost 16, I was branded with the label of slut/slag/whore. There was even a rumour in school that I had an STD!

I felt hurt, tormented and betrayed by those I thought were friends. Often in my dorm at night, I would silently cry myself to sleep, forcing my face into the pillow, suffocating myself for as long as I could, hoping that I wouldn't wake up in the morning. It felt nothing I did was ever good enough, or anything that I did do well at would be cruelly twisted into something others could hate me for.

I gave up caring, and so accepted any form of attention that came my way. If they were going to say that's what I was, why not just be it and live up to it?

I gave myself away, falling into the trap of giving people access to my body, without any respect for myself or without any consideration of any associated dangers. I was torn between wanting to be accepted and trying to escape the numbness I felt within. Only to feel even more empty and angry at myself.

My time at school became tougher. I was detached from long standing friends. Having to swap rooms and share sleeping dorms with girls that weren't in my usual circle, I reclused further. Feeling unwanted, unaccepted, a liar, a problem. Hearing a constant resounding remark that drama seemed to follow me, so I must be the problem. I hated myself and I hated school. I would either sit alone, or with teachers at mealtimes. Humiliated and rejected. I found myself spending as much time as I could alone in my room reading, or using the boarding lodge gym, in the cellar of the girl's block, usually alone and channelling my emotions into workouts.

Looking back, it pains me to say it, but I just wanted to die, to cease to exist, to release whatever burden I was putting on to people. I thought about the many ways I would do it. Then I began to discretely self-harm, stabbing my hands with little nail scissors. Trying to hold my breath as long as I could, lying under the water in the bath, or holding my face into the pillow at night. I remember one night lying in bed, lights out, attempting to strangle myself with the necklace I was wearing. How that seemed a viable option I don't know, but it made me feel better none the less.

Now I feel so sad about the fact that I thought to be accepted, liked, or in the least acknowledged, I had to share my body, but also that I just gave in so easily and just became the negative image that was made of me.

This then had a knock-on effect with meaningful relationships, especially with the ones where I really wanted to feel but struggled. I would disassociate or feel triggered, which put a strain on the relationship. I found it hard to really trust, believing that I wasn't worthy of love and appreciation, that they just wanted something from me. Why would they be interested in me? What else could I offer that was worthy? I felt that me, just as I was, wasn't enough. So, I built up walls, in fear that everyone had some sort of agenda or wanted to hurt me, and some did. I shut myself out emotionally from the outside world. Pushing people away. Having total disregard for my safety and wellbeing. I was binge drinking and having sex with people I didn't even like, but it was a welcome distraction, and was a mix between tricking myself that I was wanted and numbing the fact that I didn't really care.

Going through the tough time I did in school, just wanting to lay low, keep my head down and stay off people's radar, I would often find myself volunteering for extra hours in the art block. It was a little paint, turps and clay-filled sanctuary for me, in times when I felt I had nowhere else to go. (*I went to a weekly boarding school for military children, so I was there Monday to Friday. It wasn't that I was trying to escape home.*)

At the beginning of my final year in school, my art teacher retired. I was gutted! Her replacement was lovely, but we didn't have that rapport and special connection I had with the previous one. I would still go to the art block, but it lost its spark a bit. Taken over more by the students that weren't so good, so needed that extra support to do the work. The ones who didn't really want to be there, but had to be. And so, my safe haven became a place of tomfoolery, smart remarks and *"Don't swing on your chair!"* I would sometimes receive compliments on how good my work was from the "popular" kids, although I couldn't help but sense some sarcasm or something disingenuous in their words.

I scraped through my final year of school. Between the bullying, horrible rumours, strained friendships, a deployed parent, a very ill mother in and out of hospital, and looking after my two younger siblings, I lost focus on my studies. I remember meeting with the careers officer and being asked, *"What do you want to be?"*

I had no idea. I'd had early hopes of becoming a teacher, but I knew my grades would be shot to shit and I'd have no hope. I liked writing, and I was good at art. I remember being given a VHS to watch, all about becoming a journalist. It sounded great. But I was left feeling *meh*. It didn't feel aligned for me. I returned the VHS and told them it wasn't right for me. By this point, I'd just lost hope. Life as a starving artist didn't seem like a very successful or viable route (Oh, the irony!).

At this point, my dad was currently deployed. There were 3 months of just me, my mum, sister and brother. I became a bit of a tearaway....I say a bit, because I was still in that mindset of conformity and being the good girl, but I'd began to be led astray. I was being finally recognised by the new popular kids that had been posted to our area. I was invited to hang out with them, in fact they'd even come to the door for me. Living in Germany meant I could legally drink at 16. So, we'd often sneak down to a bar in the village, drinking half pints of Warsteiner for 1 Euro, or better yet, going to the shop, getting bottles of orange bier for 29c each, then returning the bottles for recycling to get 25c back. The drink was gross, but at 4c a bottle, who was complaining! I began drinking more and more, then venturing further, heading into town for the nightclubs. Being "cool" because I went clubbing. This became another escape for me - drinking, loud music, dancing and being whoever I wanted to be.

I was so emotionally detached from school life. I made friends with "squaddies" (young men in the army), often meeting while out in town or at events on camp. I found it easy to interact with and join in their banter. I felt accepted. And so, I made the decision…I was going to join the Army!

I started fitness training, in the hopes of preparing myself for my RFT (Role Fitness Test) and basic training. Alas, it was short lived. My Dad returned home from deployment.

"Over my dead body are you joining the Army!"

And that was that. So, I was back to square one. Who was I going to be and what was I going to do?

On one of my many philosophical, late-night chats with my dad, we had a frank discussion on the topic. We concluded that I should just study what I was good at and enjoyed, and just go from there.

The school year ended. I left school, awaiting my GCSE results. The results were reflective of how much I struggled in that final year of school. The previous year being predicted A's and A*'s in the majority of subjects.

My highest grade…B. What the fuck?!

I got a B in art and I was devastated. The ONE thing I felt I was good at and I felt like I'd failed. To anyone else, a B is nothing to be sniffed at, but I was heartbroken. I received a list of B's, C's and a D. The D in maths, which to be honest, was much better than I'd anticipated. I was, and still am, absolutely shit at maths!

So, school was over, and I felt a sense of escape. A weight lifted. But now what?! I hadn't applied to college, and desperate to get out of school, I hadn't enrolled to stay there for Sixth Form. I decided with my parents that I would stay in Germany with them for another year. Filling my time babysitting for money, being there to support my mum when dad was away. Also drinking, drinking and more drinking. The inner downward spiral continued.

After taking a year out, I moved back to England in May 2007 to settle in, ready to start college in September. I quickly made friends, and became a regular at the local pub. My drinking and reckless behaviour continued. However, I was devoted to my studies during the first year of college. I was so pleased that I was able to study art, especially as it was my 'thing'. I felt so grown up and responsible. Although, I must say, I was NOT a favourite of any of my lecturers, I was never sure why, and still not, which knocked my confidence, not feeding my need for approval and commendation. But I kept on. At this point I'd made a great group of friends - one of which I'll tell more about later in this book - which gave me the drive to keep going.

My first year came to an end, and by this point we had experienced all the different aspects of art and design we could study; it was then up to us to choose our specialty for our second year. The choices were 'Fine Art' or 'Fashion and Textiles'. 17-year-old me jumped at the chance to study fashion! I'd had received a distinction in my fashion unit in year one, so it seemed a good choice too! But to this day, I still wish I'd opted for fine art. So, the college year ended and the summer was mine.

I took a visit to Inverness to spend a couple weeks with my grandparents. Usually a good influence on me, but me, plus summer, plus a big city equalled lots of opportunity for drink and destruction. I was out as often as I could be. I was just about to turn 18, but was passing for 18 already, so got into all of the nightclubs, able to continue my binging on a mish mash of cider, alcopops and vile tasting shots. During my time away, I'd gotten a new hairstyle, lots of new clothes and felt like a new, better version of me. I couldn't wait to get back home and show everyone how 'cool' I now was.

I travelled the long journey home from Inverness to Newcastle by coach. Eager to get out to the pub with my friends, I arrived, grabbed my suitcase and went straight home. Rather than unpacking first, I hit the drink. The next morning, keen to put on my new clothes, I opened the suitcase to find some old scabby bras, dirty baby grows and a whole bunch of clothes that were not mine. I was devastated. Not only was my suitcase full of my new stuff, but also my 18th birthday gifts from my grandparents. Despite me contacting the coach company on numerous occasions, I never did get my suitcase back *(only compensation of less than half of the contents total worth)*. So back to college in September, I should have started my new fashion year feeling confident and dressed to impress, but because I was more interested in heading to the pub, I'd ruined it for myself. Instead, I had to use what little money I'd got for my birthday to buy what I could. I wasn't impressed with myself, or my look. And so, I started my second year of college, specialising in fashion and textiles, with a less than fashionable start.

I also continued on with the reckless drinking, terribly complemented with reckless promiscuity. It wasn't even a vice, just an escape and an attempt to feel wanted. Even though most of the time I felt the complete opposite. Waking up in different bedrooms became a bad habit, but one I couldn't quit. Just a few months after coming out of my 2 and a half year long 'first love' relationship,

I had even more of a 'don't give a shit' attitude and other people's disapproval only fuelled me more.

Mini Epilogue:- Since I began writing this book, I have enrolled on a Shamanic Womb Apprenticeship for my own womb healing, but also so I can elevate who I am and what I offer out into the world. This is something, at this time, I am currently still moving through, though up to now I have only moved through 4 'womb gates' (out of 13). However, I have moved through so much healing for myself, my womb, my yoni, my ancestry and more. I've found a deep connection with my womb-space and am gifting Her the love, healing and devotion that She deserves, and should have always received. I acknowledge that my past is part of my journey, but that it does not have to cloud my present or future. I now am the me that I always was, and I am thankful to the past versions of me that got Her here.

You Get to Be

She gave her body so willingly because it never really felt like her own.

The choice taken too soon for her to really be in control and know how it feels to give willingly.

Disassociation confused for confirmation.

A body she resides in, but was already taken away,

She lives there paying high emotional rent.

A shell carrying a broken soul.

With only a beating heart, she hopes one day can heal.

Time goes by and she never forgot.

More pieces of her being taken without a fight,

The lack of fight confused for willingness.

A disconnection to her body,

A body used by too many, adding up the numbers.

But each one only makes her number.

On a road of self-destruction, though not on purpose,

She has given her body in a way society expects, even promotes, yet also casts aside, shames and brands a whore.

She dimmed herself, she gave herself, she succumbed to the pressures of trying to be what she thought was necessary.

She was never fully healed, but she chose to love herself, to stop being the image she felt she needed to project.

She fully embodied her true self, her beautiful self, she said YES to being her.

She recognised she was a beacon that the world needed to see, to be shared with, in the most beautiful of ways, not in the way she was unwillingly shared before.

That she was more than just a face, a body, a void.

With her ability to love herself, unconditionally, she became magnetic to the ones who would also love her unconditionally.

Who would be there for her, to hold her, to see her, to hear her.

To let her know she was never alone.

Though you may feel broken, hurt and bruised, you hold a beautiful light within you,

A light that needs no saviour apart from yourself.

You hold the power.

You hold the key.

You get to choose.

You get to BE!

The 'A' Hole

(Trigger Warning- includes experiences of domestic abuse. Feel free to skip this chapter if you wish to)

A couple of months into my second year of college, I was keen but was in over my head. To add to the mix, now being 18, I started a new job, working in a bar. It was only meant to be part-time, but I'd ended up working over 30 hours a week, oftentimes until the wee hours of the morning. I was knackered and would often have to spend most of my wages getting a taxi home, or hoping one of my workmates would offer me a lift. It was a lot working a fulltime job in a busy bar and juggling my studies. One night after a late shift, I was tired yet super hungry and I headed to the takeaway. In the queue was one of my friends from the pub. Quite drunk, she wrapped her arms around me. *"Lauraaaaaa!!!!!"* she shouted. *"Come with me tomorrow! I'm getting my nipple pierced!"*

Well, tomorrow was Saturday, and I had the day off, so yeah, okay, I thought.

"You have to get yours done too, though!"

I paused, I panicked. Then…

"Fuck it! Let's do it!"

So, we met the next day, got our nipples pierced, high-fived each other, said goodbye, then went our separate ways. Short and sweet, with a very lasting memento!

As I walked back through the town, I passed many shouts and hollers from the many bars and pubs. It was especially busy with the 'Derby' game between Newcastle and Sunderland being on. In the North-East, it's a big deal! I headed for the bus station, trying to keep my head down and avoid the footy fans.

"Lauraaaaaaa!!!"

I looked up to see my friend's boyfriend. (He regularly gave us lifts to college, so we were pretty friendly with one another). He was standing outside smoking with his friend - one in their Sunderland shirt, one in their Newcastle shirt. The guy in the Newcastle shirt had something about him - the one that wasn't my friend's boyfriend! We got chatting and they invited me to join them. Why not! It seemed like fun.

This guy was funny and charming. We seemed to just click and were chatting for ages. In fact, it was literally hours. I was invited back for a party. We continued chatting and I feel so seen. Engrossed in conversation for hours, late into the night. We shared a few kisses. But as the early hours crept in, it was definitely time for sleep. I stayed the night, we shared a bed, but all we did was cuddle. I felt held and respected. In the morning he made me coffee and breakfast. We swapped numbers. The next day I was to be at college, but I agreed to go to his house afterwards. From then on, we were inseparable. 18-year-old me thought this was 'the one', a whirlwind romance! I was head over heels, especially with this being my first adult relationship. He has his own house, a stable job, and was the nicest guy!

Then, due to reasons beyond my understanding or control, I had to leave where I was currently living. And so, after only about a month or so of seeing each other, I moved into his place. It was fun and exciting. Now I felt like a proper adult couple living together. Although at this point, I was still at college, and also trying to hold down my bar job. The hour-long bus commute didn't make it easy, especially when my shifts were usually a 2-3am finish, which would leave me stranded, begging for lifts or having to stay somewhere until morning. I'd had to change my shifts, mainly to daytime or earlier finish shifts, causing friction at work, which eventually resulted in me having to leave before I was officially sacked on New Year's Day.

I had no income, other than the £30 a week I was receiving for going to college, which was used for my bus fare, and what minimal food I could afford. I remember scrimping up 70p for each morning so I could get a little pot of porridge, in the hopes that it would keep me full for most of the day until I got home. Financially, we really did feel the squeeze. I became a burden, unable to support myself. It caused stress and strain on the relationship, and within 3 months of me living there, it turned abusive. It was already quite emotionally abusive, but from here it quickly became physical.

At first, it was just the odd push and shove, then throwing and kicking things at me, grabbing me and digging his fingers in. Soon enough though it escalated to me being pinned down in bed with his thumbs trying to gauge my eyes out, just because I'd said the wrong thing or breathed in the wrong way. Oftentimes, I would take the hit for his own wrong doings, then have to pretend to accept his sorrowful apologies when he begged me to forgive him for being such a piece of shit.

Out of all of the many times he'd hurt me, one always sticks in my mind. It was New Year's, and we were staying with my parents. By this point, it was well known that after a few too many drinks, he would wet the bed, so this wasn't the first time I'd woken up in a pool of his piss. (A previous time, when I was on crutches because of my knees, we stayed at his family's house, and he told them it was me that peed the bed because I couldn't get to the toilet in time - so I had to just accept the disgusted reaction from his family). But this time, we were staying at my parents' house, on a blow-up bed on the floor. Once again, I awoke to that familiar warm, wet, urine-soaked feeling, already knowing it wasn't mine. I attempted a few times to wake him up, until I finally succeeded. I tried to use a soft, gentle voice, trying not to annoy him, but also so as not to wake everyone else in the house. But he woke up, already in a foul mood.

"You need to get out of bed and clean yourself up." I whispered, as I stood leaning down over him.

"Do I fuck!" he angrily whispered, as he shoved me backwards.

"I can't believe you've pissed the bed again, and at my parents' house!" I whispered through gritted teeth, a mix of fear and embarrassment.

Next thing I know, I'm pinned to the wall, his hand around my throat. His hot, alcohol ridden breath was in my face and his other hand suggestively raised. At this point, I'm feeling a combination of fear, but also relief - I am in my parents' house!

"Go on then. My Mum and Dad are in the room next door. All I have to do is shout." I uttered as I tried to get my words out, his hand still firmly around my neck. He threw me down onto the urine-soaked bed as he once again told me to clean it up. At this point I was done trying to argue, so I went to get towels, stripped the bed sheets and took them down to the washing machine. We then went back to bed, on top of various towels, snuggled up together as if nothing had happened.

I made a point of getting up early, so I could set the washing machine away, but my Mum was already up and on the case. She asked me what happened. Of course, I had no option but to tell her he'd peed the bed - I just left out the part when he had me against the wall by the throat. Then, in his true style, he boldly walked down the stairs and sauntered into the living room, arms out wide, a big smile on his face.

"Here comes pissy pants!" he shouts and laughs, as my dad laughs along with him. It's all a big joke. He takes the witty banter about it from my dad, then they sit and watch the football together. Meanwhile, I'm mortified at the fact that he's pissed the bed at my parents' house, and that he felt it was okay to treat me this way while my parents were in the room next door. So here we were, New Year's Day. A call came in from my boss asking why I wasn't at work, despite me already being previously told by another manager that I wasn't needed that day. The conversation ended with, *"It's probably best you don't come back in again then."* So, there I was, still reeling from the night before, trying to put on a happy face for the family celebrations and now jobless.

Eventually I managed to get another bar job locally, but again, it was a late finish, working with intoxicated nightclubbers and often getting attention from the punters. This didn't go down well, but we needed the money. What else could I do?! Then, again, the job opportunity was slowly dwindling, having to 'call in sick' or blag an early finish, became tension at work. My boss was less than impressed, but I had a great team of work friends that were looking out for me. After months of being hurt, humiliated and restricted, tired of having to lock myself in the bathroom, and hiding to escape until he calmed down. Tired of having to maintain the facade of being a happy couple. Tired of rarely being able to go to work or college because I 'wasn't allowed'.

Tired of having to lie to my tutor, friends and family that I was ill. I decided I was worth more.

Even though I almost failed my college course, I scraped by, managing just enough to submit a successful application to study a foundation degree. This was not gladly received, at all! I was met with a mixture of anger and sadness, being told that I was ruining our relationship, that I was going to leave him for someone else, that we couldn't afford it …. any reason he could think of. Our fights became more frequent and more violent, regularly being pinned to the bed, his thumbs pressed into my eye sockets, being hit and kicked, and objects thrown at me. Yet I worked so hard to keep up the happy, maintained view that he was great. That we were happy.

My luck changed when one of my work friends, who had an idea of what was going on at home, told me of a house share where there was a room soon to be available. I didn't know what my plan was, but I knew I had to just go for it and figure out the rest later. So, I agreed. When he was at work, I packed up as much of my stuff as I could, and I left, taking with me what I could manage, with the intention of returning with someone safe to collect the rest when I could. It didn't go down well at all, but I was out of there. I was away from his constant belittling, abusive behaviour.

I didn't give him any details of where I was living, yet, in a small town, I was constantly in fear of bumping into him. But at least I could finally breathe! I was free!!

A few weeks later, I started my Fashion Design foundation degree. 19-year-old me felt like I had really achieved something, for myself, by myself! At this point, I felt proud, I had made the conscious decision to save myself, to escape, to start fresh. A new version of me was born!

That said, I wasn't really free. I still continued my self-destructive behaviour, binge drinking, staying out late, with no care for my safety and sleeping with whoever. Returning to that version of myself that was drowning out the emptiness that still resided within. After one semester at University, I dropped out of my foundation degree. It wasn't working out for various reasons, but I guess deep down I knew it wasn't the right path for me.

From here, I continued bar work, while living on minimum funds, just trying to get by, yet continuing my path of self-hate and destruction. I was spending time with people I shouldn't, drinking too much, and doing an array of things without much regard for my personal safety. I was hurting myself because I wanted to feel something. I wanted to feel something because I had been hurting for so long.

*Mini Epilogue:- This is an experience still viciously etched into my being. Despite all of the inner work I've been doing for so long, I still find myself defaulting back to the unnecessary apologies, nervously pre-empting conflict, and feeling constantly in defence mode - even *though I don't have to. I consciously know that I am safe, and more so that I CAN handle myself, but 19 year old me is still in there clenching to what she can to remain. And, despite me being a self-confessed 'bad ass' that knows she can tackle what the Universe throws at her, anytime I return to the North East, my gut wrenches at the fear of the possibility of passing him in the street, the thought making me nauseous and the idea of making eye contact with him again sending shivers through my body.*

Spiked

A common misjudgement is that girls 'like me', bring it on themselves. While I was often vulnerable, there have been times where I wasn't typically vulnerable, where I initially was in control, yet was still preyed upon and victimised. No matter how careful we may be, how trusting, how confident, there is always a big bad wolf, and so the sooner people stop victim blaming and shaming, and hold these 'wolves' accountable and shame them, the better!

The first time I was 'spiked', I was 19 years old. (Yes, the first time! There were more!) I'd moved out, just left the abusive relationship, and moved into a 'temporary' flat share. Thankfully, I became good friends with my flatmate, and there came an opportunity to rent a new flat together above a dentist in the town's high street. A great location to be for a 19-year-old who was finding her feet and enjoying herself. At this point, I was working two jobs, one during the day in a pub not far from the flat. The other was where I was a "shot girl". They are women who wander pubs and clubs, are scantily clad, offering up flavoured vodka shots in a test tube shaped container for a few quid. Yup! I was one of those and started working, dressed in next to nothing. We were told to dress revealing and provocative, as the more flesh you showed, the more sales you made. Now the thought makes me shudder, even if I did have a pretty good figure back in the day! I would usually do the same club each weekend, unless my manager decided he needed me elsewhere. He would pick me and the other girls up, drop us and our stock off at where we needed to be, then pick us up at the end of our shift and drop us off home. One night was a particularly busy night, so another girl and I were working a bar together.

"Hey! Alright darlin'! How are you doing?!" shouted a voice.

It was my landlord. I politely said hello and he offered to buy me a drink. At first, I said I couldn't as I was working, but he insisted. I thanked him and agreed to a blue WKD. (*We could have the odd drink while working, but obviously couldn't get drunk. Back in the day I was a pretty seasoned drinker, a blue WKD was just like fizzy pop to me, so it seemed like a good choice as I knew it wouldn't have any effect.*) I thanked him again and off I went, chatting to familiar faces. Dancing my way around as I made my way round the bar and dancefloor, selling shots. I'd been so busy; I'd only drank half the bottle by this point. "*Here ya go darlin'!*" I heard as I was handed another blue WKD.

"Oh! Thank you!" I'd said as I took the bottle while he smiled at me and went back to sit with his friends. The girl I was working with, 'J', stood with me for a chat.

"*Here, have this, I won't drink it all.*" I said as I poured some from the new bottle into the old bottle, so we had a bottle each. I gave her the rest of the new one I hadn't yet drank from.

"*Cheers!*"

Off we went again, selling shots, pushing our way through the dancing crowds, and bobbing away to the sound of funky house music. I had a bit of a headache, but thankfully it was near the end of the night. The music was loud, and I was tired. My feet hurt from the giant heels I was wearing. Fairly normal. Next thing I knew, I needed some fresh air and a sit down. I went outside to the deck and pulled up a seat. I felt dizzy and sick. Maybe I was coming down with something? Then, a hand on my shoulder.

"*Alright darlin'? You don't look so good!*"

The landlord again.

"*I'm okay, I'm just tired.*"

"*Let me take you back to the flat. You'll be alright.*"

"*I can't, I'm working. My boss is picking me up soon.*"

"*Ah, fuck him. Come on, I'll take you back.*"

I hadn't been paid for my nights work yet though, and needed to let my boss know my sales, takings, etc. I couldn't just leave. By this point the landlord was sat with his arm around me as I could barely see straight, almost ready to throw up. The deck around me spinning. I'd only had a bottle and a quarter of blue WKD. I could hold my drink so I thought it must be a tummy bug.

"LAURA! What are you doing?!"

It was my boss.

"J called me, she's not feeling well, I think we're done for the night anyway, c'mon.."

I felt the landlord's grasp around me tighten.

"Laura, come on!" shouted my boss.

I tried to stand up, but the landlord pulled me back down. My boss took a step closer.

"Come on Laura, time to go".

I tried to stand again. This time the landlord grabbed my arm tightly.

"You'll go when I fucking say so! Now sit down!"

I started to panic.

You live in MY flat. I own you!"

Next thing I remember being pulled between him and my boss. My legs gave way and I fell to the ground. My boss then disappeared.

SHIT! FUCK! SHIT!

The landlord was stood over me...

"I'll take you home now. I have keys to your flat, remember!"

I didn't have a tummy bug and J wasn't ill. The landlord had spiked my drink, which I had shared with J!

"Get back!" came a voice from the door.

My boss had come back! And with two doormen who grabbed him away from me as I was helped to my feet.

"I've got a key remember!" I heard him shout as I was helped away. I fell into the back of the car; J was already sitting in the backseat with her head in her hands, barely conscious. I don't remember much of the journey home, but I remember having to call a friend who came and stayed the night with me in case there was an unwelcome visitor trying to let themselves in during the night.

The police weren't interested when we called the next day either. Thankfully I never had an encounter with the landlord again. I'd managed to avoid him at all costs, even when I moved away from the area. My friend still stayed there, maintaining our tenancy and moved another friend in, so I was able to leave without needing to see or make contact with the landlord.

But...

I wasn't so drunk that I didn't know what I was doing - I was working and had (pretty much) one low alcohol drink. I wasn't flirting with him. I never even hinted. I was a naive 19-year-old just trying to be polite. He was a 50 something year old man who knew exactly what he was doing. Granted, I was dressed in revealing clothes - but this doesn't NOT equal as an invitation, or as permission!

The second time I was spiked (not so long after the first!)...

I'd gone out to town to meet a friend/old boyfriend from school. He was in the RAF and was staying locally in the area while on a training course. We met up at the agreed location, which was a busy bar in the centre of town. It was great to see each other again. He was with a group of workmates who seemed fun, and instantly welcomed me. We had a few drinks at the first bar, we danced, reminisced; it was great fun. We moved onto another bar, you know the ones with the light up dancefloor and cheesy, good old music. The cocktails were 2 for 1, so we had a couple each. Then onto the next bar, my favourite place, who played the best house music. I was dancing with the group and my work mates had bought me a couple of drinks, I was having the best time. I spoke with a few people I knew. Between going out there often, and working in the bars, I knew many people.

I remember the heel of my shoe sliding sideways and giving way to me falling on the floor. *'Whoops, silly me!'* I thought. Shortly after I fell again. I was so embarrassed. I'd had a few drinks, but I wasn't *that* drunk, was I? I remember falling again, the weight of my body hitting the ground. Then, nothing.

I awoke, bright sunlight coming through a window, a window I hadn't seen before. I was in a room I didn't recognise, lying in a bed I didn't know, in my underwear. As I awoke and began to shuffle, a voice…

"Morning beautiful."

What the F…Who was this?! I turned, expecting to see my school-friend. But the face I was greeted with was not the one I expected. A vaguely familiar face, one I knew here and there from the town. I wasn't even sure of his name.

"You were in a bit of a state last night, so I rescued you." he said.

I thanked him and he put his arm over me. I was still pretty out of it though. Next thing, he was on top of me. I just lay there, barely able to move, without the energy to resist, so I said nothing and did nothing.

Afterwards, he passed me my clothes, and led me out in the hallway, showing me where the bathroom was.

"Remember this?" he asked. Though I couldn't remember a thing, nothing was even remotely familiar.

"That's the living room, we both sat in there chatting for ages last night. And here's the bathroom, you spent a while in there!"

Where the fuck was I?! I still had no idea. No recollection of even arriving here. Apart from the unconsented sex, this guy was being lovely. Did we do anything the night before? Had I given the impression that I wanted to?

As we left through the front door, we were in a rather fancy apartment building, all glass panels at the front and shiny marble effect floors. Brand new by the looks of it. As we walked down the stairs, he asked if I recognised anything yet. Nope! Still nothing. At this point I was a mix of feeling confused, violated, embarrassed, lost and ashamed. He drove me home, silent most of the journey as I tried to get my bearings. I thanked him for 'looking after me' as I got out of the car. I walked through my door and burst into tears. I had no recollection of what happened to me. I ran myself a bath, washing myself as I sobbed.

Once I'd got myself together, I'd messaged the guy from school. Asking him what happened, where he'd gone. But I never received a reply. All I had was a polaroid of us both together in my handbag, taken in the club, my pupils dilated. I barely looked like myself.

There have been other instances after this where I've been spiked. One at a friend's wedding, another while out locally with 'friends'. But luckily, these times I had my man to look after me and keep me safe. In my younger years, I was naive and too trusting, an easy target, but I do wonder, *"why me?"* What makes me such an easy target for spiking? Why do they even want to? These experiences have shaken me, especially knowing that this is a common occurrence in our society, which has become a 'culture'. This is my personal experience. But there are many others like it, and many are much worse!

This is why women are wary. This is why we take precautions to stay safe. This is why we cross to the other side of the road. This is why we hold keys between our knuckles. This is WHY! This is why we feel the constant need to watch our backs, to always be on guard.

"Not all men..."

Not all men are predators, but some men are!

Not all planes crash, but some do - and on that pretence they provide life jackets and safety instructions "just in case"!

NEVER judge a woman for taking precautions to be safe just in case! NEVER feel silly or over the top for just trying to stay safe!

Not all men...but some do! Better safe than sorry!

It's not only women that are victims of spiking, but this is also a problem regardless of gender. We ALL have to be wary as spiking is becoming more and more prolific and anyone can be targeted. The answer, it's not to be more careful, it's not to dress less revealing, it's not to drink less.... it's simple - DON'T SPIKE! However, until people stop being predatory assholes, these precautions have to be taken.

**Mini Epilogue:- There's a teeny tiny part of me looking back and screaming to 'do something', but, there is literally nothing I could have done. But equally there is nothing I should have to do anyway! There's not really much I can elaborate on, apart from the emphasis to remain vigilant - even though we really shouldn't have to!*

Special Connections

You know when you meet someone, and you just click?

Well...not instantly. Perhaps a few resting bitch faces, blank stares, or perhaps circumstance getting in the way, but then, when you click, the rest is history. I can owe this happenstance (I now know it wasn't) to two very special people in my life. People who have come into my life, have supported me, motivated and inspired me, been there for me in the roughest of times, and with their influence, have changed me for the better.

Let's do this chronologically.

That first special person to come into my life.. let's say it wasn't love at first sight. It was the resting bitch face stares from across the table, the awkward silences and reluctance to forcibly work together. But then came a dark, dry humour remark that would cement our friendship forever. (I wish I could tell you what it was, I just remember the uncontrollable laughing and feeling of being so understood and seen). It was there that the true

Soul sister bond was realised and began. Studying Art & Design at college in September 2007, I first connected with my best friend in all the world, Beth. (I told you I'd tell you more about '*that friend*')

Affectionately known as "Possum", as we would start and continue to call each other.

I could write a stand-alone book on our shenanigans over the years, but for this book, I'll try to keep it as concise as possible.

I can't even begin to tell you what a positive impact this friendship has had and continues to have on my life, who I am as a person and who I aim to be. Over the years I have felt so inspired and motivated by our friendship. I've been opened up to new ways of thinking, to feeling like I could pursue and further embrace my love of arts and crafts, to feeding my interest in history and culture. I truly think that Beth has hugely contributed to who I am as a person today. But not just the contribution in terms of hobbies and interests, but to find someone who will see me for who I am and hold me in high regard unconditionally. Someone who will listen to my troubles and will feel safe enough to share her trouble with me. To empathise with each other, to share our common grounds, and to share our differences. A beautiful friendship where we can express how proud we are of each other, but also know that we can call each other out, but with love and best interests at heart.

Every person deserves this kind of friend. The type of friend that is there through thick and thin. To laugh with, cry with and enjoy life with. These are the bonds we should strive to have in our lifetime. Not the ones that are conditional, of convenience or fleeting. But the bonds that will stand the test of time, the unconditional, unspoken connections. A person you can share with and know that you need not fear judgement, yet will tell you straight, although still with love. The person who has your back, and you have theirs. The bonds that don't need daily tending to, but you know that they are still there as strong as ever. A deep sense of trust. A space of love and laughter, but also where stories can be shared, and words spoken without the need to censor or hold back. A bond where you are valued, encouraged, loved, seen and appreciated just as you are, flaws and all.

Beth is this for me, and me for her. I can only hope that you will experience this special type of bond in this lifetime. Yet, had we not just shown our true self, said what was said at the beginning and shined our light unapologetically without holding back, we would never have made this connection, and instead just look back on each other's existence as previous college classmates. And so, this is the importance of truly embracing and embodying who you are. Granted, I wasn't in a place of alignment and happiness at that time, but even so, it was that part of my true self that shone through and enabled that connection to take place. So, you need not be living your highest, most aligned life to attract your tribe. In fact, it is often in the darkest of times that we are greeted with these connections. Whether they are lifelong, or only around for a short space of time, we are gifted the people we need in our life. Even if you aren't in a place of full embodiment, being unapologetically who you are, here and now, in this space and time, is how you will attract your tribe. Not playing a version of yourself that you feel is required or requested, but stepping forward, emanating your essence and being your true self as you are in that moment in time.

I will state though that your current tribe may not be your forever tribe, and equally your forever tribe may not be your current tribe. This can and probably will result in hurt, feelings of loss, and big shifts taking place. You see, when you fully step into being your true self, the self that your Soul came here to be, that acts as a filter. Filtering out the people who are not aligned to your highest good or will support you in your Soul mission. And then act as a beacon to those who are meant to be part of your life, who will have a significant impact on you and your life, in the best of ways. But our human self and our egos will feel that deeply and personally, questioning why this person has hurt us, or why we have felt a certain way. We may feel triggered or experience deep emotion. Have we done something to affect this person in any way? Should we be looking inward to ourselves? What can we learn from this connection?

It's important to remember that, when you are living from that place of alignment and embodiment, you won't just be attracting the happy, sunshiny, rosy people that we can love and hold hands with. We attract in the people and experiences needed to move closer to and to fulfil our Soul mission.

To this day, Beth is my constant in an ever-changing world. Someone who is there for me unconditionally, who knows and accepts my quirks and downfalls, and vice versa. We know that if I don't reply to a message for a week, it's not ignorance or being rude, it's just who we are, and we hold space for that. I was absolutely honoured in 2022 to be Maid-of-Honour at her wedding. And should the day ever come, she will be Maid-of-Honour at mine. I love you Possum! Always and unconditionally.

My wish for those of you reading this book is that you have already found your 'Beth' or will soon find them! I truly wish for you to know and experience such a beautiful and unconditional friendship and connection that not only inspires, but you can call your safe space. Where you know you are seen for who you are, without compromise, and accepted wholly.

When we think about connections, relationships, and finding "the one", it seems there is meant to be some grand plan, a "click", or fate. However, for me, it was a set of perfectly lined up circumstances that led me to him.

When I reconnected with someone from school years later, I was thrilled that this guy who was considered the "popular, hot guy", a few years above me in school, said he thought I was gorgeous, and that he wanted to talk to me and get to know me again. I was living in a state of dazed nostalgia, thinking how amazed and perhaps jealous friends from school would be that we had started dating. Despite distance, (he was in Wiltshire, while I was in Yorkshire) it was a bit of a whirlwind. We travelled to visit each other, meeting each other's friends and family. I visited him more, as I loved Wiltshire. It was always a place that called to me; a place that I'd returned to time and time again. He had a great set of friends, ones I fitted in with, felt accepted, and had fun!

But alas, he was not "the one". After just 6 months, the relationship came to an end. I was gutted as we had so many plans for the future. I was due to move down to Wiltshire, but also, this was still during my modelling stint, and had planned to attend a car event in the Autumn. A few weeks passed and I carried on, gutted, but determined not to dwell on what could have been.

"Hi, how r u? Sorry 2 hear about u and X."

These were the words that would shape the rest of my life. A message I received from one of his friends. We had chatted on numerous occasions during my visits, having great conversations, laughs and a shared great taste in music! It was also nice for someone from that group to reach out to see how I was. Also, he wasn't too bad on the eyes either! From there, we chatted more and more. Which then turned into long webcam chats via MSN messenger. I then decided, as I had no other plans, that I would visit for my birthday and spend the weekend together. Nervously, I caught the train to Wiltshire, worried that my ex would see us together and assume that this was something that had been going on much longer. This weekend only cemented our connection. And from there it blossomed. I remember my heart skipping a beat every time a text or call from "Tricky xx" would appear on my Blackberry screen.

Over the following months, we visited each other, which led to me making the decision to move to Wiltshire. No more hard goodbyes, miles apart and late-night MSN chats.

It wasn't without its challenges, but I do believe that has only made us stronger. There were times when we could have just walked away. In fact, there were times when we had called it quits, but when you know, you know, and the powers that be must've known we were meant to be together. Relationships aren't always meant to be easy, (*equally they shouldn't be so hard and cause pain*), but this relationship has seen us both grow together. From the 19-year-olds we were when we first met, full of life, ready to party, carefree, to the 30 something year old we are today, not so full of life, but full of love, and more so ready to tuck in early for a movie and snacks rather than to party!

So, he is my "one". The father to my two babies, the love of my life. Over 13 years from that first weekend, we are still madly in love, and I wake up grateful every morning to share this wonderful life we've created together. On the days when I can't, he does. When I'm down, he lifts me up, makes me laugh, gives the best hugs, and loves me unconditionally, flaws and all.

I love you, so very much, Marc Trick!

Mini Epilogue: - At this point of writing the book, I can only emphasise what I have already written in this chapter. If you are 'lucky' enough to have met those of your Soul tribe already, hold them dear. As time passes and I get older, I become more and more grateful for these sacred and special connections. Marc and Beth, I love you both unconditionally, in very different ways of course! I couldn't publish this book without the mention of another Soul tribe connection. I've known her for a few years already, but over the past three years, and more so over the past year, a wonderful friendship has blossomed. Lex, my 'artner' in crime, my art studio buddy and someone I hold very dear to my heart. I'm so grateful for this friendship and connection. A fellow artist and creative, but also an all-round beautiful person that I am extremely grateful to call a friend.

Not Everybody is Your Friend (But They Are a Lesson!)

It's important to realise that, where there are these fantastic connections, there are often the ones that are not so great!

A hard truth, but essential for your growth - not just spiritually, but in general. It can often be hard as an empath, as we just want everyone to be happy, to get along and everything to be all rosy. This can transpire into overpromising and helping in ways that we don't really want to but feel we have to say yes to when we really mean no. Also, in trying to see the good in people and situations, or to continue our kindness and generosity to people who should have lost that privilege long before now. Here, that people pleasing aspect rears its head too!

But because you are such a kind, loving, generous person that wants to do good, we naturally assume, or at least hope, that others will do and be the same. But alas, this is not true. I have spent countless times asking myself or wondering why someone has been so spiteful, hurtful or has complete disregard or lack of respect for others. And while there may be reasons, they are often ones that I will never find out. Rather than turning bitter with a *"fuck the world"* attitude, which so many people do have, I don't choose to view life from a victim mentality, with a *"the world is out to get me"* attitude. Shit happens, but it's how you respond and react that is important. The saying *"hurt people, hurt people"* can often be true, but I've been hurt many times, as you've come to know so far in this book. I don't set out to hurt people, not purposefully anyway, and even if I did, I'd probably fail miserably because I'm just shit at being a terrible person.

However, I digress...

We live in hope or with the belief that not everyone is all bad. While, on some level, that may be true, what's truer is that not everyone has good intentions, and not everybody is your friend. This is where discernment is key, and, I'll be honest, you may not always get it right. That's okay, you're not supposed to have everyone figured out, but equally, you don't have to approach every connection with caution. The hard lesson I have learned is that some of the people that I have praised and/or trusted the most have been the ones to have stabbed me in the back the deepest. The ones that I have told all to, trusted completely, befriended and loved unconditionally, and yet that has not been reciprocated or even respected. Maybe for a number of reasons: their own hurt and trauma, deep wounds, jealousy, intimidation, whatever it is, which is a projection. I know for a fact it is because of nothing I have purposely done to them. Perhaps very bold of me you may say, but I can hand on my heart say I have never consciously and purposely treated anyone with such a lack of dignity or respect. They may have wrongly read into my words or actions or perceived me through their own tainted lens. But again, this isn't my doing.

Much of my life was spent ensuring that people liked me, that I did all the things to people please, to not rock the boat, and not to cause upset or offence. But in the past few years, I've come to learn that other people's comfort and happiness is not my responsibility, nor is making sure that they like me. I won't lie, it is painful to find out that someone dislikes you or thinks negatively, but you have to come to the realisation that this is just life. You are not for everybody, and everybody is not for you.

Although….and this is where is gets murky…. you may meet people and feel that instant spark or connection. You believe that they are a Soul friend that's been waiting in the wings for you to happen across them at the right time, and now you have a dear friend that means the world to you. They inspire you, you have so much in common, you can empathise deeply with them. You feel seen, heard, understood, and are taken in by the romance of this wonderful Soul connection. I will state again that this is where your discernment comes in. However, at this stage, being swept up in the fun of a new friendship or relationship, or just hoping that this really IS a connection you've been waiting for, could cloud your judgement, so boundaries are an absolute must from the get-go. I wish I'd known this sooner!

But setting, enforcing and also maintaining boundaries is much easier said than done. It can be so common to push our own boundaries, either at the beginning of friendships or relationships because as a tribal being we all have the in-built desire to belong and be accepted. When you feel much comfortable and trust that person, you bend the boundaries, internally telling yourself it's an act of love. But the truth is that, if this really was that loving, two-way relationship, you wouldn't have to bend the boundaries because they would accept and respect them, or you work together to set a common boundary that works for you both. That's not to say you should never compromise, but you shouldn't have to sacrifice the important things, or anything that is detrimental to your being.

In terms of that instant connection, sometimes you may know instantly when a person is not for you, and that's fair enough; it is what it is. But if you ever find yourself constantly giving with no return (and I know we don't give to receive, but friendship is still a two way street); if this connection causes you to doubt or question your ability or worth; if you find yourself doing things out of integrity or alignment with yourself; if it feels there is a hierarchy emerging; if it feels depleting, stressful, heavy, anything negative, or even a niggle that feels untoward, take a moment to stop, to pause and honestly review this connection.

You may choose to take some time to journal on this. And do it honestly, with your first instinct thoughts. Don't try to force yourself to paint a pretty picture if it's not really there! This doesn't mean you have to eliminate this person from your life unless you want to and that's what feels necessary, but step back, re-categorise your connection, and evaluate where they sit in your circle, if they even belong in your circle at all.

Here are some prompts: -

- What is this person gaining from my friendship?

-What am I gaining from their friendship?

-What am I losing because of this friendship?

-How do I feel at the thought of meeting them for coffee, etc.?

-How would I talk about them to others if they weren't around?

-How does it feel at the thought of them talking about me when I'm not there?

-How would it affect me if this connection was no more?

-Can they count on me?

-Can I count on them?

-What would I say to them right now, if there were no negative reactions or repercussions?

Seriously review your answers. Maybe from the point of view that they may not be beneficial to you, but also, perhaps from a perspective that you may not be beneficial to them. We can often point the finger, but sometimes that finger has to point at us too.

Here's another perspective -it's one thing to get hung up on being liked, but something I've found difficult is if I don't like someone...

First and foremost, let's just acknowledge that it is OKAY to not like someone! And it's okay not to have a specific reason. People will trigger us in certain ways and there will seem like there is a lesson to be learnt there, but often we find that we just don't gel with a certain person. That deep within our core there's a nope. And it's not just a sense of '*meh*', it's as if our Soul is rejecting that person's energy into our space. As a species, us humans like to analyse, to know the how's and the whys, as that gives us some form of justification or validation. But what if you can't receive someone, but you can't put your finger on it? Are they a bad person? Are you a bad person for feeling that way?

So, let's look at it from another perspective...I give you my olive analogy.

I LOVE an olive; in fact, I'd say borderline obsessed (but I didn't always like them). I know a lot of people are a HARD NO on an olive. Pop one into your mouth and you get that immediate *"BLERGHHH!!"* It's gross right? You want to SPIT IT OUT! So that's what you do. You get it straight out of your mouth and feel the pure disgust! Afterwards, do you sit and wonder why you didn't like it? Why you didn't want that olive in your mouth? Why you were so repulsed that you couldn't ingest it and you just had to get it out? Do you begin to think that you may be a bad person or that there is something wrong with you? Is the olive bad? What MUST that terrible olive have done to have this effect on you?! Fuck that olive! And now you're going to obsess over how much you don't like the olives, losing focus on the foods you actually do enjoy…

WOULD YOU seriously partake in this scenario?

Maybe you would, but I'm going to guess you said no and thought the whole olive thing was a bit daft…

*Note: - If you're actually an olive lover like me, then replace said olive with a food that you cannot stand, something you can't bear to try and eat.

Anyway, we just accept that we don't like olives, probably don't eat them again, and that's life. Maybe some time down the line we might try one again to see if our taste has changed. Or you might have one sneakily snuck into your food and you still definitely don't like them. But are you losing sleep over it? Those olives you don't like - how dare they! How dare they sit in a bowl and be eaten by other people, look at them. What have they done to MAKE that person eat them?!

Now switch that olive to a person! ...

You don't have to overanalyse why you don't like them, maybe they're just not to your taste and that's okay! You are allowed to not like someone! As empaths and people pleasers, we can strive so often to please everyone and create a happier, more peaceful world, when we just want the world to get along! So, when WE don't like someone, it can be a hard pill to swallow. We're all about that peace and love, right?! Moral of the story is that not everyone is to your taste, and that's okay! We don't have to be rude or mean to them, nor do we have to be able to pinpoint the exact reason why, but knowing when to take a step back, set a boundary or distance yourself for your own sanity can go a long way towards your happiness! Stop stressing over the worry and why's of not vibing with someone and start focusing on creating conscious connections with those who ARE your people and your tribe!

*Mini Epilogue:- The more life moves on, the more I resonate with this chapter. I've learnt to keep my circle small and be wary of who I trust. Not in a bad way, but I'm more conscious of who is deserving of my time and energy, in turn easing the social anxiety and rejection sensitivity. I do have many acquaintances, and some *great outer circle friends I really am grateful to know. However, in terms of my 'inner circle' - I could count on one hand and still have fingers left! Never get caught up in any form of popularity contest. Go for quality over quantity. I'm at the point now where I know I'm not liked by some people, and there are some people I don't like, but I'm no longer losing sleep over it, obsessing about how I can make them like me, or wondering why they don't. It is what it is, and I've learnt to be okay with that.*

Selfishness Is a Must

BEING SELFISH IS NOT A BAD THING! A bold thing to say. I must be an awful person, right? On the contrary, I'm actually a super nice person! (I promise!) These days people throw around the term selfish in a bad way, and of course there are people that do awful things that most would consider what society now believes "selfish" to be. Obviously certain actions are not good at all, but is that them being "selfish", or are they being "self-centred"?

Going back to the basics, being selfish is simply "putting yourself first". **Self-Care and Making Yourself a Priority IS Selfish!** And that's <u>not</u> a bad thing! We are now programmed to believe that putting our own needs before others is a terrible thing to do. It's actually a natural survival instinct that should be ingrained in us, but society has us believe that certain things are selfish, and that selfishness is bad. As such, we are conditioned to believe that self-preservation is a bad thing because we "must" choose to put others first, which results in so many of us being burnt out and feeling like crap. But let me take a few steps back there …. "Survival instinct" - and that's exactly what it is! If we don't care for ourselves and put ourselves first, then how can we survive?! How can we be there for others who need us?

How can we keep ourselves in a state fit to do what we need to do?

Are you thinking I'm an awful "selfish" person?

Well…. Yeah, I am selfish! But I'm not awful. I am a mother with two beautiful children, one of which has significant special needs and a higher level of required care than a typical child of his age would. The other child is of an age where she requires a lot of emotional support, and I am just being a mother in general. I know how important it is to prioritise my children and their needs, all the while still being able to prioritise myself too. Me saying to you *"Put yourself first"* is NOT me saying *"fill your own belly and don't feed your kids"*, or *"spend all your money on yourself and leave them with nothing."* etc, etc. What I am saying is, whether it is to children, partners, family, pets, friends, work or anything else that requires our care and attention - to that we do have a level of duty (after all, is that not the reason you're telling yourself that you can't put yourself first?), but it should never be to your detriment. We have people or situations who depend on us, and so we owe it to them, if not ourselves that we do look after number one, that you have that chance to recharge your batteries, that you don't feel burnt out and that you still maintain some form of self-identity.

Self-love and divine union. Why is it so important? How many times have you heard about self-love and told yourself you would make time but never did? What are your thoughts or expectations of what self-love is? Have you been programmed to think it's bad or it makes you feel guilty? Or are you able to happily practise true self-love?

It's much more than squeezing in a half an hour bubble bath or treating yourself to a chocolate bar amongst the weekly grocery shop. It is much deeper than that. It goes beyond what we can physically give ourselves and is more about HOW we treat ourselves. It's our inner monologue, our choices, our boundaries, what we are and are not willing to tolerate, to receive or do. It is about standing your ground because you KNOW your worth and will enforce your boundaries. It is having an unconditional love and admiration for yourself, regardless of external influence or opinion. It is how you nourish your body, mind and spirit.

To practise self-love doesn't require wads of cash to frequently take yourself off on spa days or retreats, although it can include that if it's within your means and vision for yourself. Self-love doesn't have to cost money. It will cost you time, but in the best possible way.

But still, what about the worry of being selfish?! Goddess forbid, huh! Worrying if people would see you badly for doing something for yourself. If they would resent you for taking time out, or away from your busy life. For spending money on yourself, when it could have been spent on more "important" things. For spending time on something for you, when you could have dedicated that time to someone else. But in that instance, that judgement usually comes from a place of jealousy, even though they may never admit it. So many people crave and only dream for the opportunity and ability to live a life where they get to make the choices, call the shots and be in control of who they are, so even if they don't admit it, the disapproval and judgement comes from that jealousy, even subconsciously. It's not necessarily that they want to do what you are doing specifically, more so that they believe we should, or have to, remain in our box, for fear of being ostracised and outcast as part of society. So again, it's not you, it's usually them. We can't help it if we trigger people by living our best life. We can just live in hope that the triggering inspires and motivates them to make better and more aligned decisions. But if they choose to operate from a place of resentment, that is not our responsibility to ease.

If we continue to run ourselves into the ground, devoting every waking moment, penny and piece of energy to everyone and everything else, how are we going to look after what really matters to us? Our children, our families, our pets, and our relationships - those important things that we want to dedicate ourselves to, not because we have to, but because we want to. If you've got zero battery left, how are you going to do those things? So, while feeling worried and resentment towards spending time, money or energy on yourself, ask yourself *"Will this help me to be a better *insert title here*?"*. A better mother, wife, partner, daughter, friend, human being!

For those that have followed me on social media for a while, you will know that one of my trademark sayings is...

"YOU CANNOT POUR FROM AN EMPTY CUP!"

And it is so true. You have the goal to support and care for everyone else, but what will you do when you literally have nothing left to give? When your mind and body just give up? It is important that you DO make yourself a priority, because in doing that, you are creating and tending to a better version of yourself. One that is not only more able, but is happier, fulfilled and also, an inspiration!

When you feel like you've lost all control and hit rock bottom again.

When panic sets in.

When you don't know how you'll cope.

When you don't know how you'll make ends meet.

How you're going to do the things you said you would but physically can't.

Don't focus on how bad it will be, or that you can't manage. Don't focus on the no's and the cant's. Focus on the **how's** - how can you overcome, how can you take the next step, how can you do the thing. Most importantly, focus on YOU! Because if focusing on you means you can elevate yourself again so you can do better to support those around you, then that is NOT selfish at all.

If you find yourself in a hole, acknowledge that you are there, don't pretend that you're not. Because the quicker you acknowledge, the quicker you find solutions, or you reach out to those who can help you to find solutions. Acknowledge that you're in the shit, but also tell yourself that you can and you will get out of it. Then be that *'FUCK*

YES!' version of yourself who devises a plan to get back to being fantastically you on the top of your game!

I've been so blinded at times by all of the bad shit going on, that on several occasions I missed the point that I've been going through a major shift. A shift where I've been flooded with amazing opportunities, alignments, or things perfectly falling into place, but have been so focused on the negative, or just feeling dragged down by all the negative things that I can't control, I've forgotten to focus on what I can control.

When things get rough, it really can feel like the weight of the world is on our shoulders. We become consumed by the pressure, the fear and the exhaustion. Then it becomes one big cycle, and as we know - energy breeds energy. I always find it helpful to take a step back, a deep breath and to take a moment to try and mentally detach from the shit storm that I am within. To step outside of the chaos tornado and assess the direction it's headed, and which direction I'm going to take. I mean, you could step right back into the eye of it and later down the line feel disheartened, more exhausted and really pissed off that it seems never ending. Or you could look at the other available directions that will take you immediately out of the metaphorical harm's way, looking back over your shoulder as that tornado sweeps pass, blissfully knowing that, not only did you step out of it in the first place, but that you didn't let it win, suck you back in, or carry you along as it caused more destruction. It can be hard to do though, I know that, for it's a difficult habit to break. But when you start to make the effort to consciously shift the mindset and perspective, to initially put yourself first, without feeling the guilt, that positivity - in terms of both energy, and opportunities - will present itself, and breed more positives to come.

Let go of feeling bad or 'selfish' for doing things for yourself. Plant seeds that will flourish into what YOU want, or will at least take you a step closer. Those around you will also be able to marvel at and enjoy the beauty of it all in bloom.

In a world where people would rather vilify two people in love, rather than vilify people spreading hatred. Where they would rather condemn a flag of rainbow colours than the killing of innocent people and animals. Where they judge a person for their difference in ability, rather than the arrogance of those who pass judgement. A world where your access is granted or denied depending on the colour of your skin or how you talk. A world where men with no business have control over women's bodies. A world where a predatory man is let off the hook, rather than the belief and support of those who were victimised by his actions. A world where likes and follows have more stature over wisdom and kindness. A world where innovation and questioning are silenced if it doesn't meet the preferred narrative. A world where you're told to be yourself but vilified for shining your light. A world where people are more invested in fictional TV characters' lives than the welfare of those who are in deep need of support. A world that is hurting its people and its own being. Pillaged and plundered, inhabited by those who seek power, riches and glory.

What has this world become?

In a world that feels like it has developed to be pitted against us, and us pitted against ourselves, always choose you in this world. It is not selfish, nor is it ignorant. Because the more we choose ourselves, remain true to our values, and who we are at our core, that authenticity echoes out, it multiplies, and it becomes the medicine that the world so badly craves. We find self-love, compassion, and open mindedness. We discover that the 'done way' is not the right way, merely the way of those who have thrust their ways upon us. Over the centuries they have conditioned us to believe it is the only way, and anybody who dares question it is punishable.

You do you, and one by one the world will continue to heal. Even if not for ourselves, but for those that will follow in our footsteps.

Let's leave a legacy of love, acceptance, understanding and awakening, and let's leave behind the patriarchal, fascist, racist, homophobic, self-centred, glory seeking ways that have damaged our world and its people. One of best things you can do for the greater cause is to step into who you are, and be that person unapologetically, for then will you embody the true power within that will give you the strength to be the good and the change you intend to be!

I surrender to being me as I am without the need to prove myself, to puff out my chest and put on a display of strength and independence. That's not to say my feelings and emotions weren't real or valid at the time; they absolutely were. But we evolve, through our life experiences, learning about the world around us and, more importantly, learning about ourselves. Just because you were one thing at one point, don't let that hold you in that space, unable to move forward. You are allowed to shed old skins. To transform and blossom. You are never bound by who you have been or what you have felt. You always have the opportunity to become more you as you ebb and flow through life. We're meant to evolve!

Even something as permanent as a tattoo can still change, evolve and turn into something better. How are you binding yourself to old ways and old thought processes? What's keeping you from really becoming you? The you that you know you really are right now? How would things change for you when you choose to become YOU!? (Not the version of you that you think the world wants to see)

Know that you are in control, and that you can and should say 'no'. Too many times I have been either left short, or caught up in something I'd rather not be, because I felt powerless and unable to say no. I felt unable to enforce my own boundaries for fear of dismissal, rejection, confrontation, or often, because I just couldn't bear to handle the hassle and backlash. To resist saying no always felt like an easy way out. But in denying myself the ability to say no, I also denied myself time, opportunities and the ability to stand in my power. So often, we applaud the 'yes' people and the 'go getters', but actually it's the 'no' people that should receive the recognition and appreciation, for they are the ones that are able to enforce and exercise their own boundaries, that know they're non-negotiable and refuse to budge on them. The ones that refuse to give away their power to someone else.

That said, whether the word is yes or no, always make sure that you do you. Stay in your integrity. Do not give away your power. Easier said than done, I know. Nobody has it to a T every time, but the more you practise this, the easier it gets. Know that it sets a precedent to those around you - that you are not a pushover or an easy target. Of course, you will likely receive some kind of negative reaction because you are not succumbing to other people's wants and expectations. This will go one of two ways. Those who do not appreciate or value you will be the worst ones, for they will be awkward, they will be grumpy, and they will lay the blame onto you, saying that you are the one being difficult. As hard as this can be to deal with, especially if it is someone you are close to, highly respect, or having been seeking approval from, because you will more than likely experience a feeling of rejection or wrongdoing, remember

"Those that really matter, don't mind. And those that mind, really don't matter!"

The moment you begin to drop the fear of doing what everyone else wants you to, and you start doing things for you, you will feel the shifts - both positive and negative. That will generate expansion for you, showing that you have no room or tolerance for less than you are with, and the Universe will recognise that, bringing you more of which IS aligned with you because you are freeing up room, filtering out the crap, and making space for what you desire and deserve. Of course, clearing out the garage space isn't going to magickally manifest a Ferrari to appear (or maybe it will?!), but what it will do is clear the way for you to have and be more. I've said it before and will say it again - energy breeds energy. So, what you give out, you get back.

Mini Epilogue: - Revisiting this chapter has only reaffirmed and reinforced what I have said, even to myself. Yes - even our own words can help us to check ourselves. It doesn't always have to come externally, you already hold much of the wisdom to support you, it's just having the trust to listen, the willingness to be the person who answers and chooses from a place of alignment, and is able to claim positive selfishness as an ingredient in the recipe that is a good life. It is OKAY to say yes to yourself and no to others!

The In-Between and the Squeeze

The in-between, limbo, that feeling of all consumed "meh"! The *"I can't quite put my finger on it"* phase. These times before spirituality dawned on me, in hindsight, were so much easier. The simple sense of 'ignorance being bliss' approach to problems, when you just felt like the world was against you and that was that. Chalking it down to being bad luck or a rough patch.

But now we have that more enlightened sense of thinking, a higher perspective, and a more awakened take on our problems. Gone are the days of simple self-loathing because life was shit. Now we question. We question EVERY. SINGLE. THING! And it is fucking exhausting!!

What is this teaching me?

What lesson am I to learn?

I'm shedding all that no longer serves.

It's clearing the path for something better to come.

And yes, while all that is true, in the meantime we're stuck in that limbo of clinging on for dear life, in divine trust that the Universe really does have our back, but wanting to revert back to that simpler time of being blissfully unaware of the notion that there is a lesson or bigger plan for us.

I often refer to the Universe as a mirror, reflecting back what it receives. Which in turn makes it more difficult, because oftentimes I want to send up a big ol' "FUCK YOU" to the Universe, but ironically, the Universe would most definitely fuck me right back, harder, while laughing in my face. And so, we muster on, receiving and receiving in trust of this quest for a greater good, for the Soul mission, awakening, enlightenment, whatever you want to call it.

We talk about shit hitting the fan and we also talk about the good times, but people rarely talk about the in-between, that lull of numbness, where nothing exactly feels wrong, but it doesn't feel right either. Then you're stuck in that space of loathing, stress and exhaustion, waiting for the penny to drop, for everything to align and say *"SURPRISE!!"*, giving us the sigh of relief where we feel validation that it was all happening for us, not to us, then off we head on our merry way again.

But how do we navigate the in-between? We never know how long it may last …. days, weeks, months? How do we not fall into that pit of despair and resentment while waiting for the good to appear?

You see, the in-between acts as a holding pen (excuse the phrase). A space where we don't move up or down, forwards or back. But we remain, and this essence of stalemate forces us to really see where we are right now. To reflect on recent occurrences and happenings. To review our vision for the time ahead. To experience the present, and sometimes painfully come to a realisation that we are within a cycle that has to change. That before we can move forward and pick up the pace again, that there are shifts or shedding to be done. But it's not so black and white. There's no instant knowing what should remain and what should be released. We have to work through it, painstakingly, really witnessing in real time what has become our reality. It gives the opportunity, and it really is an opportunity, to uncover our shadow self, to feel Her emerge from our depths within and to lay all our shit bare. And it hurts.

But know this…it is okay to feel like this. It is okay to find yourself in the in-between, without a what, where or why. You don't need to have the answers, equally you don't need to have an overwhelming sense of hope and trust. I mean, it has to be there somewhere, even in the subconscious. But it is okay not to be all sunshine, rainbows, and love and light. You are allowed to feel. Remember you are a Soul having a human experience, and part of that experience is feeling, and more often than not, feeling very deeply.

However, an extra added pressure of the in-between, is involuntarily carrying the weight of other's judgements or remarks. You see, we need this in-between time to recalibrate, to know what we feel and to realise what we do and do not want to feel. Any external sign of weakness, lack of gratitude or feelings of defeat and deflation often comes under the scrutiny of others…

"What have you got to complain about?!"

"You're lucky, you should feel grateful!"

There most certainly is another side to people's perceptions of us and what they may see. Yes, to the outside world you may be doing really well, but that doesn't always equal happiness or fulfilment. Yet you feel the pressure to excerpt some sort of gratitude, showing the world that you are grateful for all you have. Feeling like you're not allowed to feel down, deflated or left wanting more.

How dare you!

How dare you want more when you already have so much!

How dare you feel sad when you have so much to be happy for!

That voice inside your head may say these things, but it's okay to want more and to be more.

Those of us here that are becoming aware of our higher powers and soul missions know that we ARE here for more, and so it's okay to go for it. To strive to be and do more. You do not have to settle! You do not have to play into anyone else's ideals of how you should look, feel, act or behave!

If you need time and space to sit with any deep emotions, then do that.

If you have a goal or dream and you won't stop until you achieve it, then do that.

You don't have to be down and out to experience and express that you're having a tough time. You also don't have to settle for the now, to take stock of what's already there for you and think *"I better not"*, when you know there is more to be had. What you do have to do is to follow your own journey, which will never be a straight and upwards path. It's a meander of ups and downs and side to sides. But what matters is that you do it your way. That you stay true to you. That you allow yourself to feel unapologetically and express that without guilt or fear. That you celebrate yourself and your wins. That you give yourself time to feel into your emotions and to rest. There will always be someone somewhere that's worse off, no matter what, but that doesn't mean that how you feel isn't valid. Whether you're up or down, never dim yourself to appease the judgements of others.

All that put aside (The remarks may still come but becoming "immune" to it is a skill to be practised), you must know that anything and everything that you do feel is real and valid. You need not explain or dissect for anyone. The important thing is that you yourself fully acknowledge how you feel. Not doing so is just like sweeping it under the rug. As tempting as that may be, it'll just mound up until there's nowhere left to sweep it to.

You may have heard the term "Dark Night of the Soul". While I have encountered the experience for myself, I'm going to talk about something different. Rather than your whole world crumbling and falling to shit, with life as you know it from that point on experiencing radical change, I want to talk about what I'm calling "The Squeeze". And when I say squeeze, I'm not talking about the sensation when someone hugs you a little too tightly, I'm talking about feeling like you've been truly wrung out, twisted and squeezed until you feel like there's not a drop left. An experience that strips you bare and physically reduces you to a point of feeling like you are literally dying, barely comprehensible and gasping for metaphorical air - to then emerge out the other end, shiny and new, with a new lease of life, a more focused or streamlined perspective, heightened senses, a more in-depth connection, and a new-found sense of alignment, which leaves you standing there thinking *"WTF?!"*.

When I think of this metaphorically, I imagine a wet sponge being wrung out. Every last drop of stale, tepid water being let go of. Then when the squeeze releases, we expand again, ready to soak up what we need. Once again, taking the form that was intended. Not being weighed down with excess.

But that squeeze, that time when you are being wrung out ever so tightly, often happens in times of sickness or injury, usually at a time when we could really do without it happening. The timing feels terrible. But then in hindsight, it was perfect timing, for it was likely at a time when you needed to slow down, to rest and recuperate, to find the slow and stillness, enabling you to see a different perspective, or to evaluate what's what.

Much like the in-between, the squeeze is also here to help, even though it doesn't seem like it. Whether that is forcing us to stop and take it slow, or having a detox forced on our bodies, with sweats, sickness, or any which way the body can release toxins. Feeling like both our bodies and our minds have shifted, and, when you can feel deeper into your own being, reading the DNA coding shifts and upgrades.

This happened in January to February of 2023 (not the first, and probably not the last time). I was almost bed bound for at least 4 weeks. My body was weak, I could hardly sleep, but when I did, I still felt exhausted. My body was constantly sweating, and I experienced sickness and diarrhoea. During my illness, I also came on my period. I had conjunctivitis, an eye infection, an allergic reaction, a cough, and a runny nose. It just felt like one continuous thing after another. But on reflection, my body was on a mass detox, getting all the bad stuff out of my body any way possible, bringing everything to the surface to expel anything that was not to remain within me physically.

Since then, I really have felt such a shift, more in alignment, but also more attuned with my body. My weight and body shape has shifted, and for the first time in years, although I don't have a perfect body - I'm curvy, slightly overweight, have saggy skin and stretchmarks - I actually love my body now. I can look in the mirror without feeling pure disgust and resentment, and that really does say a lot! Especially after hating my body for so many years. I still have problems with rosacea, redness and dry skin on my face, which I'm sure is symbolic of some other healing that needs to be done and lesson to be learnt, but I trust that all will be well, and eventually I'll done what needs to be done for it to heal.

*Mini Epilogue: - One year later, on reflection, I had a similar experience in January and February 2024, my fibromyalgia flared terribly, and I was bed bound for a couple of days and then had to use a walking stick to get around for a week or so. It was not quite so extreme this time, but it's interesting to notice patterns and recurring instances. With this, I invite you to see if you have become aware to any regular patterns in your life, any particular time of year when something happens, what it actually is that is happening, how you feel then, how you feel afterwards. This can help you to be aware, but also *to pre-empt, navigate and learn from this recurring happening.*

I Didn't Know I Was

"I'm afraid someone will whisper in my ear while I'm asleep."

Sounds eerie doesn't it, but it was the words spoken out of my own mouth.

Let's go back....

I've always been intuitive, but when I was younger, I didn't know I was intuitive (the realisation came much later on). I always felt weird growing up; I knew and felt things that didn't make sense. I would see things that I was so sure I had seen and experienced before - to the point I was able to tell my friend the next sentence our teacher would say before the words even came out of his mouth. I would hear noises that "weren't there". I would see shadows that "weren't there". I would "imagine" lots of faces at my window, staring at me, watching me trying to sleep. I would hear whispers in the dark. And so, I developed a coping mechanism of having to cover my ears whenever I go to sleep. I would also get very anxious about having curtains open if it was dark outside. I didn't know that this wasn't normal. I didn't know that not everybody could see and hear these things...mainly because

I didn't talk about it much to know any different, but I didn't see it as much to shout about. I mean, would you go around shouting and telling people *"I can see the sky!"*? Well, of course, you wouldn't because in your mind, you're sure that they can too, so why should it be announced? And so, I didn't really think any differently about it, except for the fact that I was a bit weird and had a very creative mind.

However, when I got older and into my late teens, I finally realised that I hadn't been aware of my "abilities" this whole time. I'd just thought I was a bit crazy and oversensitive. It hit me like a ton of bricks about all of the stuff I had experienced from a young age. I then realised this wasn't normal; far from it in fact. I had been accessing higher information and communicating with higher beings the whole time, I just didn't know it! From there I began to explore and deepen my knowledge and my practice.

At 19 I got my first tarot deck. I hadn't known much about tarot, readings or energy work before that point. The closest I'd got to any "woo-woo" awareness was my obsession with watching *Most Haunted* in my teens, as well as holding 'made up' seances and trying Ouija boards. I was always surprised that when I tried it, blindly without a clue, it seemed to work. I had also seen and heard a lot of "ghostly" activity in my home too. But apart from that, the spiritual realm was an anomaly to me.

By chance, the place I was working had hosted a ladies psychic night, and I was invited to join and had my cards read. The reader told me that I had the "gift" and needed to start exploring and using it. After being told that I had 'the gift', I would pull cards for friends "as a laugh", and then we would all sit around astounded that what I'd said was true. If it wasn't at the time, we would weeks later come to find it had come to fruition.

I wasn't confident in myself at this point. I thought it was a novelty or a party trick I could pull for friends, but would somehow always work, and work really, really well. I never read the book or any information on what the cards actually meant. I just went with what I was drawn to in the cards and how that made me feel. I never took it seriously though. In fact, there is a photo of me in front of a card spread, legs crossed in a "meditation pose", mocking myself. I wasn't aware that this would become a way of life, and that there is so much more to leading a spiritual lifestyle. I would joke that I was psychic, not realising what it really meant and that I was very psychic and in tune.

Growing up I hadn't known or met any psychics, mediums, or other energy workers (not knowingly anyway). The closest I'd got was avidly watching *Most Haunted!* I was a mega fan! Could you imagine my teenage self finding out that in years to come I'd be one of the *Friends of Derek Acorah's* guest readers!

In my early 20's I'd had some guidance on growing my skills, but I'd begun to explore more and teach myself. In turn I was becoming more confident in what I could do, and, in the information I was receiving. From then until now it's been a long journey, exploring different spiritual avenues, years of practice and skill building, also building my confidence too. Trial and error of not only finding myself, but embracing who I am, the me without the social moulding and external pressures. A big part of my journey has been loving myself, not just for my good points, but for what I'd perceived as my flaws. It wasn't easy, and I had to work through most of it in hiding. This was due to a mixture of being afraid to reach out to ask for support and not knowing who to reach out to. The knowledge and skill I have today is a culmination of self-study, personal experiences, practice and exploration.

I could have really used a "me" back then though! Despite trying to find a solid mentor, I was either left disappointed, or without any more of an idea than when I started. It can be a hard journey to navigate, not only if you're unsure personally, but there is so much conflicting advice, bitchery and judgement. It's a spiritual war zone out there!! Here we are, trying to navigate our own upleveling, empowerment and spiritual journeys, while juggling the multitude of life tasks at the same time. Questioning ourselves.

Are we doing the right thing?

Are we doing something wrong?

Are we appropriating?

Are we bypassing?

Are we settling?

Are we too much?

Are we too little?

Are we manifesting hard enough?

Are we meditating deep enough?

Are we clutching crystals strong enough?

Are we witch-ing enough?

Are we yoga-ing enough?

Are we channelling enough?

Are we wafting sage wafty enough?

Are we inserting yoni eggs deep enough?

Are we initiated enough?

Are we grounded enough?

Are we fucking levitating high enough?!

When will we ever be enough?

It's become a joke and a competition of who knows/does/feels/says/manifests the most... and it's a shambles! So, it's no surprise that, as we attempt to navigate ourselves, we are constantly feeling triggered by outside information. We are perhaps still feeling triggered from inside information too. So, let's approach each other with a bit more gentleness, be that in our personal or professional roles, spiritually or otherwise. The spiritual industry has become a minefield for catty do's, don'ts and 'absolutely do-fucking-nots'.

Enabling and empowering others to see things from a different perspective or point of view is one thing. But grabbing them by the metaphorical face, while holding their eyelids open and forcing them into the mirror to see what is going on is traumatising in itself, and it sucks! How can we genuinely and confidently go within, to dig deep and really see what is going on with us, when we're trying to resist a figurative claw in the eye and an externally forced headbutt to the mirror? There are other ways to look within and embark on "the work".

A message I channelled, that I've sat with and journaled on personally:

"You don't have to be drowning first before you can learn to swim".

Basically, you don't have to wait until the shit hits the fan, until you fail, or until you're struggling before you can learn, or seek help. Do the thing when you want to, not just because you need to. Reach out to those you trust, seek recommendation, but maintain your own discernment, lean into what feels like a yes and what feels like a no, with practice and with people. There's no point trying to force something if you know it's not for you. But what if you don't know it's for you? Here's a little practice I like to do with the people I work with, so they can move forward with surety that they can recognise their inner pull.

Recognising a full bodied 'yes' and 'no': -

With your journal to hand, come into sacred space with yourself.

Focus on your breath, letting all around you melt away. Focus on the inhale and exhale, feeling the rise and fall of the chest, listening to the air entering and leaving the body.

Open all of your senses up to how your body feels.

Place a hand on your heart space. Feel the beat of your heart, and also feel into how your emotions are held within the chest.

Place a hand on your womb space, feel into any sensations you may experience, and feel into how your emotions are held within the womb space (whether you have a physical womb or not, the space will still hold your womb energy).

To enhance your physical awareness, using both hands at the same time, touch your thumb on the tip of each finger, pinkie to index, and then back again.

When you are ready, placing your hands wherever feels most comfortable, ask yourself:

"Show me what a full-bodied NO feels like."

Be with yourself, feel into any sensation, emotion or experience. How does your body and mind feel in this moment?

When you feel that you have a clear indication, journal fully your experience, even if anything seems odd or obscure.

Then once you've journalled, shake off your whole body as if you are shaking off dust.

Then follow the process again, but ask of yourself:

"Show me what a full-bodied YES feels like."

Again, journal your experience.

Having a knowing of what these feelings are like, you can tune more into decision making. Even as you go about your daily life, being able to feel and recognise what these yes and no's feel like. Trust your instinct too. This can also help you to reinforce your boundaries.

*Mini Epilogue:- It is here, looking back that I realise how valuable the spaces and opportunities I provide are! One of my life missions is to be the me that I needed, in many ways, and in this instance being the safe space and mentor for women, facilitating the safe sanctuary to create, grow and forge strong connections with myself, the world around me and also to know unconditional loving connection with other like-minded women. I am a space holder, and I take great joy and honour in knowing that I have and continue to support many women (and children) in having the opportunity for self-love and exploration.

Stereotypes and Surface Level Spirituality

I often think back to that starting point where I had no clue, no respect for the cards and no idea that this was barely even scratching the surface. Even now, when I use the word "spiritual", I am faced with strange looks, fingers posed into crosses or people asking if I talk to the dead. That just reinforces the collective lack of awareness of the spiritual and holistic. Recently it has really become more mainstream and widely accepted, which is great. More people are awakening, and also, we are realising this is not a time and space of fear and persecution. But waiting in the wings are still those that cast us in bad light. The sceptics and the non-believers. The misinformed or the mislead. The scammers and the charlatans.

In every profession and trade there are always dodgy ones. But when you do energy work, the bad often outweighs the good. It's our human nature to be cautious of the unknown. Add that to hundreds of years of patriarchal, witch hunting, heresy, punishing, indoctrination, views and actions, and you've got a lot to contend with. The world isn't so kind and accepting to that which are different or not understood. And so, I found myself in a space of trying to prove I was the real deal, but trying to also arm others with the know-how of how to spot a scammer or make a more informed choice of who they were parting their money with. It didn't mean they had to come to me, just to be discerning in who they were not only paying but letting into their energy.

It is mine and many others rule of thumb that you do not offer an unsolicited reading, spell work or healing. Those who need it will find us. And so, I urge you not to fall victim to this, no matter how convincing they seem, or what they say they have to tell you. Also, be wary of names you know and trust. I say names, not people, because there are so many fake accounts out there on social media, posing as people who are the trustworthy ones. If in doubt, just say no, even if you really feel like they are genuine. Do your research. But also, before just deciding to book, perhaps ask yourself why and what it is that you actually need, so you can make the best use of not only your time and money, but also your energy. And if you have been scammed, do not let this rest on you as a reflection of yourself. I have been scammed, more than once, and by trusted names. So even if they are trusted, ask the questions - ask the what, when's and why's. Any genuine service provider, regardless of what they offer, will always be upfront, open and honest with you. This is also why transparency is one of my key values.

Anyway, continuing on my own journey ....

Offering tarot card readings and messages from spirit, I would relay predictions from the cards and give messages from loved ones. People would come to me for a reading, I'd tell them what I had to tell and then that would be that. They'd go off on their way, then usually sometime later get back in touch to tell me what I'd said had "come true". Great! That was validation for me, and for them. I went from strength to strength with my readings, and became very good at reading cards, tuning in to my intuition, and then also connecting with spirit. I've lost count how many readings I've done over the years, but I am grateful as some of those have really connected me to some special people that have been a big part of my life. I was getting great reviews and word of mouth quickly spread. At this point I was only charging £15-£20 per reading. This was just a side gig for me, alongside bringing up two toddlers at the time. I was cheap, but accurate, and so people would book a reading *"just to see what it was like"* or *"for a laugh"* or *"just for fun"*, and at that time that was okay, as that's all I classed myself as, "entertainment". I progressed from just 1-1's, to doing house parties, small events and then intimate psychic nights, of up to 40 people, at various local venues. My prices increased to £40 per reading. I was receiving great recommendations and my diary was fully booked. I was THE most recommended psychic medium in my area. My diary was chocka with 1-1's and events.

I was then asked to do tarot cards at an Arabian Nights themed function and was requested to come in fancy dress "like a traditional fortune teller"....I declined.

It was from here that I realised that this was a joke to a lot of people (not everyone), a bit of fun and that there were no real benefits to my clients - apart from feeling like they needed to hear where to go and what to do, or to have a message from someone in spirit. These people weren't committed to me and what I did, but rightly so. There was no real reason to invest in me, to truly believe in me or to feel like my work had given them more than just a bit of fun or excitement there in that moment. Don't get me wrong, I did have a handful of loyal clients, whom still to this day stick by me and my work and have always seen my true worth. (You know who you are, and I wholeheartedly thank you. You saw me and my worth before I did and I know there are those of you who will vouch for the support and transformation I had given you, back then and up until now.) I also think that speaks for itself, that even though I stepped back and took a break, I still have a large handful of loyal followers who have stuck with me since the very beginning.

And then I stopped and gave it all up. I cancelled any bookings and events I had lined up, turned away requests for new bookings, as much to the disappointment of many, I closed "The Psychic Peridot".

This leads me to share the 3 (main) reasons I gave up being a psychic medium, and why I would never go back to it again!

Firstly, before I go any further, let me just clarify, this is NOT me discounting or saying anything untoward about psychic mediums. They have a valid place, and there are some very good ones out there!

This is just why I, personally, chose to stop being one.

1 - Testing & Sceptics

In any role, where you seek to be recommended and do a good job, there will of course be judgement and expectations, but for me, being a psychic medium took that to a whole other level. Aside from just being able to focus on doing my job and doing it well, it felt like a constant jump through hoops, proving my worth, defending my integrity, and appeasing the sceptics - those who would expect me to request crossing my palm with silver and tell them they're going to become very rich and meet a tall, dark handsome man, or they would ask the most popular question,

"Tell me the lottery numbers."

To many, it just felt like a complete joke. An opportunity to project their own shit onto something else, because they didn't have the understanding, respect, or even the want to understand on the most basic of level. They would just judge because of the engrained, societal stereotypes.

Then was the weight of expectation. I always delivered with transparency and honesty, but sometimes for people that wasn't enough. There would be those that would hold out for that one golden nugget of information as true proof, and if you didn't give that, all other accurate information would be irrelevant. It felt like a constant battle of having to defend myself, while doing my best. I became tired - tired of trying to show the world I wasn't a charlatan, and being categorised as someone who takes from vulnerable people.

Not just being judged by strangers, but often people I knew. They would react in jest, but I knew it was just a gentler way of telling me that they thought it was all bullshit.

It also created inner and outer conflict for me, questioning myself and feeding my anxiety.

It really took its toll, which led me to...

2 - My Physical Health

I'd already been diagnosed with chronic health conditions and so my health wasn't the greatest, but the above affected me mentally and physically. Aside from that, when I connect in with spirit, I feel, physically and emotionally and it becomes draining, at least it certainly did for me. Feeling the pains and sensations within my own body of those who'd passed really affected me, which would then often flare up my conditions and I'd need at least 3 days just to recover from doing a reading. I couldn't not feel during a reading either, as it was one of my main clair-senses, alongside seeing and smelling, as well as just knowing. I will say my clairaudience (clear hearing) wasn't my strongest skill, so rather than just being able to relay words, which is what most people wanted or expected, it took extra work to interpret the information I was able to receive. So not using that sense of feeling wasn't a possibility, especially as that would be a key indicator for me in indicating how the said person in spirit had passed. It was also a strong element of validation and recognising who it was that my clients needed.

Then, lastly ….

3 - I'm Not a Show Piece

I was aware that this was what I was in a sense. I'd always list that my readings were *"for entertainment purposes only"*. This never really sat right with me, but it was what I had to say to ensure I was adhering to the correct advertising rules. I knew that I wasn't here just to entertain, I was here to make a difference, real change, support and to be a part of something bigger on a soul level.

The final realisation for me was when I was invited, in fancy dress, to attend an Arabian night's fancy dress theme event and be their "fortune teller". It cemented the feeling I'd had that I wasn't being taken seriously. That, even though feedback I'd had was often that I'd given closure, confirmation, validation, hope, etc. to many people, that really I wasn't doing much more than telling them the what, and not giving them the how. Also, it would often serve as a "band-aid solution" for many because that's what they needed to hear, but not implementing anything, and coming back months later, in the same situation or headspace, wanting to just be fixed, rather than given the tools and know how to do it for themselves. There was no real client accountability, and I couldn't help to generate the deep support and positive change I knew I was here for.

And so, I stopped.

Everything.

I cancelled and refunded bookings (including a public audience evening) and took a full step back. I needed it personally for myself to recoup and heal, but also professionally. I knew this wasn't the path for me and my whole being knew that too. But just knowing that wasn't enough, I had trusted and acted upon not only my instinct, but on what I knew I needed and what was in MY best interests! Regardless of the mountain of disappointment seen through the lens of praise of how good I was, and also through the guilt of cancelling bookings and letting people down, it was an important lesson - it's better to put yourself first and let others down on your own terms, rather than keep pushing to burn out, temporarily pleasing people, only to eventually still let people down anyway.

And so, I stepped back from my readings to spiritually and energetically hibernate. I began to dig and explore my spirituality deeper. It was during this time that I took up yoga, began to meditate more regularly and invested myself in deeper spiritual practices and learning. I began to see what was truly out there on another level. What I could really do and what I could access with my intuition. Another world and another way of being opened up to me. I learnt to fully embrace who I was as a person. I found myself and learnt to openly become and show who I had been all this time. Before then, I was so worried of stereotypes, of being perceived to be a certain way - social anxiety had been rife for me up until this point. But now I was stepping into being myself. I started to dress the way I wanted to, instead of dressing more "conventionally" like I had done. I became more vibrant, inside and out, I was no longer embarrassed. People knew me for the real me, not some public friendly persona, and in being myself I gained true friends, ones with similar interests. These were my kind of people, my soul sisters.

At this point, I was just scratching the surface, yet to discover higher frequencies, spirit guides, angels, deities, soul connection, ancestral patterns, past lives, and much, much more. I was on the precipice of something amazing and I didn't even know it. Nor do many others. Those who claim to be "spiritual" often cruise through on shiny facades of crystals, tarot cards and/or a connection with the dead, without ever digging deeper. I was one of those at one point too, so this isn't me just pointing the finger, but bringing light to the fact that some people are unaware of the wealth of wisdom and information out there. Some don't need or want to and that's okay, but it's like buying a car without having a driving licence - you have everything you need to get you places, further places, to explore a world of beauty and enlightenment, except the actual know-how of how it works, and so the tools and fancy bit become redundant. There are those who do practise mediumship and readings, but also have extensive knowledge and experience of 'the bigger picture'. These are the types of people I personally would seek guidance from because it's not just about entertainment or quick fix readings. There will be more depth and understanding of energetics, of frequencies, beings, even healing and perhaps even deeper types of connection and soul work.

Unfortunately, the part of spirituality that is often judged or stereotyped is the surface level, the 'glamour', so it is no surprise that many choose not to venture any further, or even take the time to begin to understand it. But there is much more to explore, enjoy and grow from - finding purpose, stepping into your divinity and coming into full embodiment of self. It seems a self-injustice for one to dip their toe in the spirituality pool and then not delve any deeper. It's like looking at something through a keyhole and making decisions based only on what you've briefly seen. Then there are those who make up their minds without even gazing through the keyhole but have been conditioned (through generations) and repeatedly told to believe what is on the other side is bad, mainly by others who've not even gazed through the keyhole either. An endless cycle of people with no true reality or experience, pushing their views and distaste on others, pointing the finger at anyone who dares to explore and find out for themselves. And we're the bad ones?!

So, as I continue through this book, I'll be not only tempting you to peek through the keyhole, but to fling open the door, step in, and take a journey of self-discovery and deep connection that takes you way past the surface level spirituality hurdle that many stop at. That said, this is not a 'how to' book. My hope is that this is a book of self-connection and discovery through my own story, which also gifts you opportunities for reflection, inspiration and motivation. I want it to serve as a checkpoint and help you to be discerning about where you are in your own path and where you aim to be.

After doing a lot of my own inner work and really finding myself, I decided it was time to open back up to offering my intuitive skills to others, but with a higher energetic, more meaningful level. I didn't want to be considered the novelty I had done previously. I wanted to be able to provide real guidance and transformation for my clients. Something that wasn't really done with my previous work. I wanted people to truly believe in me and see that I was worth more than just a bit of fun, and that I could support real change and enable them to feel more positive. I wanted to help others to feel seen and heard, to be able to facilitate their own transformation, and, with guidance, to be able to create and follow their path.

I was already an accomplished artist, offering portraits and teaching adults and children. I was used to sharing my skill and knowledge. Teaching and mentorship were certainly a calling for me. I trained in meditation, healing and spiritual life coaching, combining with the skills I already had, knowing that there was more for the world to learn, to unlock and to achieve, I stepped into the role of being a messenger and a guide, joining the clan of soul sisters calling people home. I am not just a psychic medium, I am an artist, an intuitive, a healer, a mentor, a guide, and a channel for the divine. I offer myself with the highest intentions, with compassion, with empathy, and with a real hunger for genuinely supporting the people I work with. I am not a novelty. I am not "just for fun". I help to unlock the positives within, and to support you to become your true self. I invoke the parts of you that you've either forgotten or didn't know were even there. Not just through guidance, but through soul art, meditation, healing and mentorship. I am not the only person out there that does what I do, but I am the only me. I am my own unique combination, and I want to truly thank you for seeing that and choosing to connect with me and to trust in me.

Always remember to step into who you truly are, regardless of fear or judgement. If you are yourself then at least you will be seen as the real you. We often worry that we are being judged, but really, we are not. Our public persona is being judged, and all too often we pander to that and feed it more. Take off the mask and step forward into your true authentic light. It is then, in your own true energy and appearance, that you will have the tools to take on what you need to. Trust in yourself and those that matter will too!

*Mini Epilogue:- Further along the line, I continue to look back, grateful to myself for the decisions made in my 'spiritual' path, but also realising that it's not all spirituality. As a 'label', spirituality has been a big factor for my transformation, and still that word creates unease in some people, but at the heart of it, what it really is, is true connection to self, the land and the energy around us. Using *that to weave various threads throughout the fabric that is our life and being. That's not to make it more palatable for the non-believers, but to make us realise that we can't always surrender the credit to external forces. We need to acknowledge that the power mostly comes from within, and it is us that is the centre piece for our change and uplevelling. Whether it be tarot, meditation, holistic therapy, mediumship, whatever it may be, is the tool, as long as it supports us to be a better version of ourselves. It doesn't matter what the 'tool' is, it's the result that is key! And if people don't like us doing things that help us to become a better person then that's on them. Although the caveat is that we shouldn't be doing something or using a 'tool' that isn't aligned with us, only doing it just because we feel that's what we should do. Do what feels right to you, and let go or move away from what doesn't! It's all part of the learning journey.*

Finding Your Flow

"It's murder on the dance floor. You better not kill the groove"~ Murder on the Dancefloor by Sophie Ellis-Bextor

(To add that this was written some time in 2022, I had no idea that this song would resurface in a popular series and become a viral hit again in 2024!)

I danced to this song in front of the whole school. A dance routine I had choreographed and taught to friends. In fact, one of many routines. I would often hear a song and visually start putting together a routine in my head. I was hugely big on dance and loved to get others involved in dancing with me - often to the detriment of the adults around me as they'd be forced to watch shows and routines.

That all came to a harsh stop around age 14. I was diagnosed with juvenile arthritis and suffered pain in my knees and hips. I would have to sit out of P.E. lessons, which to many I guess would be a blessing, but at this point I was very active, mostly joining in team sports. Having to sit on the sidelines while my classmates' played rounders was always a metaphorical kick in the face. Sports stopped. Dance stopped. And so, one of the things I was so passionate about came to an abrupt end. No more dance routines for me. Although I would still find myself moving to music where I could.

Prior to this I had two loves - art and dance. The dancer in me faded away and my artwork took precedence. So, to many I am Laura - the artist. Never Laura - the dancer.

Skipping a few years, to age 24, I received a new diagnosis of Fibromyalgia and Joint Hyper-Mobility Syndrome. For months after that, I was a zombified version of myself, dosed up on a concoction of meds, and barely conscious. I gained weight. I was in so much pain, my emotional state was pretty much down the toilet! (Adding in my son being diagnosed with ASD during this time too). Then I rediscovered my love of art, despite the arthritis in my hands setting in, I could still hold a pencil, not only well - but very well!

From there I started a pet portraits business, and it was booming! Once again, art had saved me. Mentally, emotionally, and had given me more financial freedom, not to mention hugely boosting my confidence and self-worth. Fast forward again to not quite now, but a couple of years ago. I was at a point where I was able to manage my chronic illness. I've since developed the work I teach, to be a fusion of all of my loves, art, dance and spirituality. I'll never be the dancer I aspired to be, but the fusion of movement and creativity within my spiritual work is something I truly cherish. Not only has it supported me in finding and loving myself and developing further on my path of spiritual confidence, but it has supported many other women to do so too.

It is often thought that to be creative you must be a good artist. And while [tooting my own horn] I am a good artist; you don't have to be!

Creativity is much more than slapping some paint onto a canvas and making it look pretty. It's much more than choreographing the perfect dance, more than writing a beautiful song, and more than filling pages of a book with touching words.

Creativity is something that lives in all of us, waiting to be explored and unleashed.

Creativity comes from within, in many forms. Creativity holds infinite possibility. It holds the key to getting from where you are now, to where or what you desire to be. In its simplest form, it is the spark that glows, growing, until it illuminates a pathway, a process, to lead you to the desired destination. You don't have to be able to be stereotypically creative, you just have to have even at least some small part of you that wants to do and be more than you are right now. As well as knowing that that's not selfish or self-absorbed. It is when you awaken and embrace your creativity, in its deepest and truest form, that you can really begin to carve out the path, and step towards the life that you really want, but more importantly, the life you came here to lead.

I always feel that while creativity is somewhat a thought process, but it truly begins in the body, down deep in the Sacral Chakra. An ember, patiently burning, waiting to ignite and set your world ablaze - in the best ways! And so, connecting in with the body is key. Really feeling into and getting familiar with the body that your Soul resides in. The divine temple that is home to your Soul self, your essence, your sacred being - which is why we should treat it with reverence, love and respect. Embracing all of it, even the parts that our egoic self doesn't love. Or in some cases has come to detest.

We'll come back to the devotion to self later in the book, but back on to the subject of creativity. It not only comes in many forms but produces many forms.

What have you done lately that has had some sort of desired outcome?

How did you get to that point?

Did you make a plan of sorts?

Did you "wing it"?

Either way, there has been some level of creativity involved, whether subconscious or not. My aim, for myself and to share and awaken within others, is to really come home to that part of yourself, to unleash that creative fire within, nurturing the Sacral, deepening into sacred creativity and sensuality. Connecting all parts of you back together, into wholeness, so you can emerge as the woman who CAN have it all.

I don't mean the stereotypical fancy cars, flash handbags, mansion houses, Louboutin's and so on. Unless that is your goal, then why not?! But if you want to cultivate a life of abundance, in various forms, to breathe each moment in pure joy, happiness and fulfilment, knowing that you are not only at peace, but thriving and continuing to do so, then stepping into that is going to take your creative self to really step in and step up.

I can guarantee whatever your passion is, was or will be - it involves some sort of creativity, even if it seems unlikely. But that passion will often also be your safe space. Where you feel like you can escape the weight of the world, to really be in a state of oneness, where, maybe just for a short time, everything feels okay.

For me, that safe space was art. Drawing, painting, crafting. Even going through a stage of wanting to be my own Editor in Chief of a magazine…the one I would create with a wad of printer paper, stapled together, with crudely drawn editorial spreads and wonky crosswords. Whatever I was doing, I'd be all in, lost in it for sometimes hours. For me, it was a safe haven to escape the pressure of real life. A space where I didn't need to feel accepted, where I wouldn't be judged, or held accountable to anyone else's ideals. I could just float away in my own mind. Sometimes this would be gorgeous painted landscapes, places I wish I could travel to, copies of photos of my family, or most frequently, my cat! Others would be doodles, fuelled by my own angst, conveying the deep sadness and worry I felt inside.

Although art was my escape and a place not to be judged, I would still seek approval and validation, desperate to show someone what I had created. To receive commendation and positive feedback for how well I had done. It was one of the few things I was really good at, so would be my go-to "praise fueller". Holding up the piece of paper, I would say, *"Do you think this is okay?"*

I was hoping for an encouraging, congratulatory *"Wow!"* To reaffirm that I wasn't a useless failure. That I WAS worthy. It didn't really matter who it was - a family member, a friend, a teacher -.as long as I got that metaphorical pat on the head, I would be content.

In middle school, my parents and I were told by my teacher that *"Laura has no artistic talents and will never amount to anything!"* In college, one of my lecturers, without realising I was actually in the room, publicly called my work "shit" to the class. Had I let these words affect my love and interest in art, I wouldn't be where I am today. Other people's perceptions and opinions are irrelevant, and often turn out to be projections of their own problems or insecurities. Maybe they were having a bad day, or going through some personal stuff, which still doesn't excuse their actions, but had I let their crap impact me, not only would I have been throwing away something I held so dear, but would also be leaving my space of solace to the wayside. In the years where art had been my solace, I can only dread what may have replaced that void had I not continued to pursue it.

Wherever it is that you find solace, safety, inspiration, the place where you can beautifully lose yourself, cherish it! Regardless of anyone's input. All too often we fall into line, but it is those of us that rock the boat, break the mould and step out of the box, that are the ones that truly make and evoke change, whether that be for ourselves, or on a more collective level. So never be afraid to make your wonderful mark on the world. The biggest regret would be to have never tried.

Despite any knockbacks of doubts you have about your level of creativity, I honestly do implore you to go ahead, to try the thing, whatever it is, because creativity is the thing that will support you in moving forward - creating plans, creating ideas, creating opportunities, all merging together so you have the drive, ability and confidence to truly craft a life you love!

Much of my work is steeped in the fusion of creativity and spirituality - including art and movement. A journey that I have walked and benefitted from personally. You don't have to be busting out big moves for this creative fusion to work. You don't even need to be entirely mobile. You don't even need to be a "good" dancer.

It's about connecting with the flow of your energy and feeling that through the body, where you can. Surrendering into that flow state and shedding skins of judgement, fear and self-image. Beautifully embracing you, in your purest form, moving naturally, either while you create a visual image of that flow, or just simply move within a safe space. Being true to you and glowing from the benefits of doing so. Literally dancing to the beat of your own drum. Feeling the warmth as it moves through your body. Reconnecting with yourself, dancing away your fears, dancing for your ancestors, dancing for the parts of yourself that have felt lost, suppressed or longing for permission. Feel the parts of your body really move, even the parts we have felt we shouldn't move and explore. Moving in deep sensuality, without feeling sexualised or objectified. Feeling fluid motion weave throughout the body, unlocking energy that had been trapped and became stale. Sending surges of joy and freedom throughout your very being.

Giving yourself permission to move is not just about doing a dance and pleasing others. It is so much deeper than that. It is a form of healing in itself. That is why I move as much as I can, when I can. That is why movement is a key part of my work in spaces I hold for others. I am not teaching you to dance, nor am I guiding you in specific movements. I am facilitating the opportunity for you to move and connect with your physical being, which is just as important as connecting with your emotional and spiritual self. The saying *"dance like nobody is watching"* carries so much more weight than you may realise. The body is the physical temple in which our Soul resides, and so we must not only treat it accordingly, but connect accordingly. We have become so disconnected from our bodies. They have become shells, hit with internal and external criticism and ground down by over physical workloads, but also not treated with the reverence they deserve.

So here, I beckon you to connect with YOUR body. Really deepen in to explore her external beauty, her internal power, the movements, the sensations, the energy that moves through. Nourish and hydrate, begin or continue a self-care regime. Perhaps treat yourself to an indulgent treat for the body.

I invite you to stand in front of a mirror and truly see yourself. Not focusing on what you perceive as flaws and not to judge, but to accept and love. To give thanks to your human vessel. To honour her, to allow yourself to see her in her purest form. Releasing any external or internal judgement or emotions towards your body. Welcoming her aesthetic with love and adoration. Explore moving the fingers, moving the toes. Rotate the wrist, move through each of the joints, feeling full bodied movement and expression. Stretch, open up the body, move the hips. Really become aware of how the body moves and how it feels in movement. Every day we move, but how often are you consciously moving?

Without pressure, restriction or control, but just exploring your own flow, from the smallest movements in the fingers, to big armed movements. Tune into what feels good, what offers different emotions and sensations. Make a note of this, which you can refer back to when you want to move into experiencing and feeling those emotions and sensations again. Feel free to use props, to lean, to lay down, to sit, to sink in, stretch, whatever you feel you want to use to support your exploration of movement.

Find Your Flow Prompts:

- Music that makes YOU feel good.
- Surrender fully to the space.
- Let your body move freely.
- Move hips side to side, bring in arm movements.
- Move hips front to back, bring in arm movements.
- Move hips in a circular motion and bring in arm movements.
- Move hips in a figure of eight with arm movements.
- Allow the moment to become more fluid, leading from the hips.
- Create space with the body and the arms.
- Shake, jump, wiggle, anything that generates energy within the body.

"When you allow your body to explore its own free movement, you shed skins of fear and confinement, and clear the path for you to experience your own sense of freedom, becoming so beautifully lost and found all at the same time" - Laura Anne

I'd also love to gift you access to a taster video from my bestselling *"Soul HeARTed"* program. It packs a punch and is full of empowerment, supporting you to find your flow, connect with your body, and creating a ripple effect as you shed skins and begin to uncover the parts of yourself you had perhaps felt lost or unloved.

**'Find Your Flow' Taster Link: -
https://anuveya.mvsite.app/flow**

Following on from your movement experience, I would also invite you to journal.

Emotionally, how do you feel?

Physically, how do you feel?

Does anything feel like it's shifted for you?

Did you experience any resistance?

Mini Epilogue:- *Since beginning this book, I have found my self-appointed 'label' of Holistic Artist, which seems so simple but for the longest time was a blank space in my mind, or a mish-mash of fancy words to create a business friendly label. But the two words work perfectly together, encapsulating all that I do and love. Art is holistic, but holistic living IS creative! Through my continued development and experience, I see just how important this is. Not just to teach people to create pretty pictures, of for me to create pretty pictures for other people, but to create an immersive experience where it awakens the Soul, the inner self and opens up a pathway for healing, inspiration, motivation and more. We need both sides of our brain for survival, it's no secret, but so many of us get caught up in the logical, analytical left-side brain way of thinking which, even if we don't realise, can be so restrictive. Enter the right-side brain. The playful, creative version of yourself, that is able to problem solve, generate more exciting ideas, to feel more fun and engaging, to increase our memory and cognitive function, and so much more. It's not just about being creative and making pretty things, it's about unlocking and utilising that creative mindset to create the life YOU want!*

You Can Lead a Horse to Water, But Should You?

You can lead a horse to water, but you can't make it drink….

So often, we look to others to heal us, to solve our problems, to give us the answers, to tell us what to do, or to just do it for us. But in doing so, we are doing ourselves a disservice.

Notice I say we and not you? That is because I know that I have done this, and still feel like I could do with someone to do it for me sometimes. But in doing so, we are giving away our power, we are disregarding our own skill, wisdom and knowledge, and we are ultimately stripping ourselves of the opportunity to learn, to grow and to build upon these situations.

How many times have you had a hard decision to make, turned to your closest ones and asked, *"What do I do?"*. How many times have you booked a reading in the hopes that you will be delivered all of the answers - the how, what, when, where, and the why?

How often do you go within when you are seeking advice and counsel? Is this part of your practice? Or does the mere thought scare you off? We forget that we hold infinite wisdom and possibility within. That we have divine access to the information that is for our highest good, and we forget, or maybe don't believe, that we are capable of accessing that.

And so, my role offers support in the way of guiding people to that remembrance. Not to tell or show the wisdom within, but to shine a light on the way there. To awaken a sense of remembrance that reinforces that knowing and the self-belief that you are capable and worthy. My role is not to tell others what they should or shouldn't do, nor is it to be the fixer, or to mend their problems. But this is where I've found it gets difficult. As a guide, people want to walk down the path of least resistance with my support and oftentimes are reluctant or scared to do the work, to experience the lows as well as the highs, and just want me to offer a way out or around it. I've done readings in the past where people had said that I didn't give them what they wanted and the information didn't tell them what they wanted to hear, only to have messages weeks, maybe even months, later that in fact what I had delivered to them, wasn't what they wanted, but was what they needed.

Equally, I've known stuff was coming up for myself. I didn't want to face it, nor did I want to believe it. In hindsight, I see now that I needed to. And so, I want to expand on the saying *"you can lead a horse to water...."*.

You can lead a horse, but it's not always easy. That part alone can take some effort, in either supporting others to believe the water even exists, that they are able, or worthy to drink it when they get there. That they can make the journey and that it's not some plan to poison them. That there may be obstacles on the way, but they can be overcome. Leading people there is probably more than half the battle! I guess that's where I come in, however I'm not holding the reins, dragging unwilling people, I'm not even telling them that they have to.

What I do is to say, *"I struggled to get there too, but I've done it now. I've walked the path. I can show you the way I went. You might need to go a slightly different, way, but I'll support you, using my own experience. When times feel tough, I'm here. I understand and I know how it feels to be afraid, to take a step forward."*

I can draw the metaphorical map from my own experience that may help you in some form on your own, or I can be the torchbearer that helps you discover and shine a light on your own map. But it is up to YOU to make the journey. You are ultimately accountable for your actions and lack of actions. Nobody else is responsible for your failures, or your triumphs! People may contribute, but that is relative.

You ARE in control, whether you believe it or not. Every situation has a choice. Even if you are not in control of the situation, you are in control of your reaction, and those actions and reactions are the detrimental parts where you get to exercise and stand in your power.

Where you get to either show that you have learnt, or are willing to learn, but are expecting others to do that bit for you, it achieves nothing. It may get the job done for now, but it doesn't support you in the way that you need it to. These unsettling recurring themes will continue to resurface until YOU learn and you do the work, breaking you free from the cycle you've been caught in. You can have all of the information and wisdom in the world, but unless you do "the thing", you get nowhere.

We are all accountable for ourselves, our actions, reactions, our choices, and our perception of the world around us. So many times, I've fallen into that mind trap of thinking that I'm the problem, that I'm at fault. I tell myself that I'm not wanted, I'm being judged, I'm being attacked, that I'm being talked about, made fun of or that others are against me. Sometimes, that has been true, but, the majority of the time, it is the narrative that's gone on in my mind that I've let take a hold over me, diminishing my power, my confidence and my worth, when in actual fact, none of it was true. Something I've come to learn is *"it's not all about you!"*. We are responsible for supporting ourselves to take a step back, a deep breath, and to remember that, although we are at the epicentre of our own lives, we are often only just on the peripheral of others' lives, never truly knowing what is going on for them, regardless of what we know, or think we know. We have to surrender to the fact that it's not about us. That we may feel uncomfortable, but this is our inner narrative taking the reins and leading us down a dark path. So instead, we must act from our sovereignty, to become indifferent, although still aware, but to release what we cannot control and to act on what we can control - our actions and responses.

We cannot control the horse being led to the water or make them drink. But we can support how we react to the horse, how we support ourselves in that journey, rather than putting our sole focus on the horse. Rather than thinking that it's our fault the horse won't drink, step back and rest in the knowing that you have done as you should (or if you haven't, then you must act accordingly to put it right). You may find out why the horse won't drink, or you'll simply never know, and we have to be okay with that. What matters the most is that you have acted and responded from the mindset of your sovereign self. That in itself is a learning journey, that you will have hopefully moved through your own lessons to be learned. Your lesson was never about making the horse drink, it's about learning how to respond to whether it drinks or not. And the horse, drinking or not, is their own lesson. Ultimately, is not our responsibility.

Mini Epilogue:- On review, as one of the shortest chapters in this book, I do feel it's one of the most powerful. We place so much external validation, blame or hope on things that we forget to come back to ourselves and view the situation from an untainted, un-victimised self. It is so important to remember to hold ourselves responsible and accountable. While others may play a big role in things, it is ultimately us that controls how it goes, how we react, and how we move forward from the situation. Even in times when it feels like you have no choice or control at all - your reaction is always a choice.

Deeply Stored Wounds

For so long, I have been both intrigued and captivated by the past - different eras and movements, places, and people. So many I have felt a strong resonance with. For a number of years, I have both been researching information on past lives and exploring my own past lives. It's a topic that intrigues me, but has also given me a feeling of clarity, healing and in some cases, closure.

More than that, past life wounds can be carried forward into future lifetimes and manifest as fears, phobias, physical and mental ailments. It can affect our personality. While many will argue that karma is not carried forward through lifetimes, there are lessons to be learned that are reflective of our past life experiences, rights and wrongs.

So many people often say, *"Don't look back"* or *"Look where you're going, not where you've been"*. But I strongly believe that we can learn from the past in so many ways, and also heal from it to either avoid happenings or to finally fulfil a mission. And so, I have delved into a few of my past lives …. there have been many! It's interesting to look back into them, to see any recurring patterns, lessons that hadn't been learned or missions unfulfilled, any reasons for my current lifetime strengths and weaknesses, as well as soul connections and bonds with others.

The Workhouse 'Guardian'

I've spoken frankly and openly in this book about ways I've been hurt and treated, mostly by men, and so it was interesting for me to discover a very prominent past life where I was a man who abused his status and power. I was a successful businessman in Victorian England. I owned factories and workhouses, was very wealthy, wore an expensive tailored suit, had tidy hair and a neat moustache. I was a tall man of average build, but had a big, intimidating presence. I was a highly regarded member of society with money and social status. I had it all, but I was a horrible man. Lower class people were 'things' to me. They were workers and I worked them to the bone, with disregard, disrespect and hatred. I especially treated women and children in abusive and harmful ways. Ways that my current self is deeply ashamed of and saddened by.

While I previously commented that it is widely said that karma doesn't carry through different lifetimes, there are obviously karmic patterns of lessons to be learned or missions to be fulfilled. As such, the Soul self needs to have these experiences, to work towards those missions and lessons. Interestingly, any past lives I've explored since that one - including my current lifetime -I have been a female who has suffered at the hands of a man. Some fatally, some in ways that are survivable but leave a deep scar.

But that was only back in that late 19th century. How many lives can I possibly have between then and 1990 when I was born?

Well, this is where it gets even more interesting...

In any of my past lives, including ones that pre-date the life I've just mentioned, I've never been 'old' or what we would consider elderly. I've never lived past 40-50 years old.

It's a known fact that, historically, people didn't live as long. However, in many of my lifetimes, I've died prematurely, either by accident or have been killed. This has left an engrained fear, worry, and unknowing of growing old in my current lifetime. Maybe this is it though. Maybe this is the time I get to grow old and finally reach and embrace my Crone self? But in the meantime, let me introduce you to the past versions of me, the ones that were here for a short period of time, and have filtered into that fear of growing old. I refer to them as:

The 'Lost' Girls

Between the Victorian man and me now, I know I have lived at least 3 lives. Which coincidentally are decades/eras that I have a strong pull towards and interest in. I was here in the 1930/40's during WW2, then again in the 60's and the 80's. All female, all killed by men, all at what is considered a young age. I've yet to delve further into two of those lifetimes, but the 1960's lifetime is one I have been working with deeper.

I was 16 years old in the U.S.A. I had been out with my high school friends and was walking home alone. I was grabbed out of sight, assaulted and killed by a man behind a diner. The name 'Christine' feels very relevant here too. In terms of geography, I keep coming back to hearing "Maryland". I have been doing all I can to research this, but it's still a work in progress, to get all of the facts and see if I can track down exactly who I was.

In doing all of the 'work' in this lifetime, I'm really hoping I can break the chain, for my own Soul self and subsequent lives, but also ancestrally for those who come after me in my family line, to free us from this pattern of abuse and harm.

Another wound and recurring pattern for many is the witch/sister wound, one that probably 99% of us carry. A product of persecution, throughout history, often in reference to the infamous witch trials, but also, going back through time, the punishment and persecution of anyone who was different, displayed some kind of 'power' or ability, or that could operate in a way that was incomprehensible to the masses, often involving stories of betrayal.

I know for sure I have lived many lives as a witch/seer/mystic, but there are two that have been most prominent in my personal past life exploration…

Rashmi - 'Ray of Light'

Dating back to Babylonian times, I was a 'seer', a medicine woman, practising herbalism and healing in my home formed from mud, sand and earthy materials. I was a gentle but powerful woman. I had long dark hair, and only one physical seeing eye. From my exploration, I learned that the other eye was injured and blinded by a snake. That harsh looking exterior played into the 'hag-like' aesthetic. I would create medicines, tinctures and also work with waters to cleanse them for safer drinking. I would often help children, but that was misconstrued, and I was punished at this point in time, not as a witch (it was before the time for that word), more so a 'sorceress'. But I mean, same thing, right?! I was tied to a stake, had my hair cut off in humiliation, because it was believed that it was take away or diminish my power, and I was stoned to death and then burned as an angry crowd watched on. I was punished because of other people's fear, insecurity and closed mindedness. I could go deeper into this lifetime, but that would be a whole chapter in itself.

Moragh ("Mo - Rag") - "Star of the Sea. Great. Alternative of 'Mary'"

Another prominent past life that I have worked with in quite some detail, and continue to do so, is another 'witchy' lifetime. My name was Moragh (Pronounced either 'mow-rahh', or 'mo-rag'), which is a traditional Gaelic name. In this lifetime, I was in Scotland, I fell in love with a 'prince'. We were running away together but he was injured and unable to venture on. He begged me to go on as the King's guards were drawing near. The story was then spun that the 'witch' was trying to steal the prince and lure him to his untimely death, but the truth was that we were madly in love, and I was carrying his child. I left Scotland and fled to Ireland. I lived in a hut in the woods, living with my daughter, making spells and herbal remedies, dancing in the moonlight, living off the land and laying low. It was a secret bliss for a while. But during this time, we were found by the townspeople who wanted us gone, amidst a time of vilifying and punishing heretics and pagans, and so set our home alight. Once again, we fled, barely with our lives. The whole side of my face was covered in scars from the fire. We returned to Scotland once again.

This is a life that has held the most hurt and resistance for me, but also the most powerful resonance. Upon another of my visits to Glastonbury, within The Goddess Temple, I received a vision which offered closure to this lifetime. I saw myself, standing atop a cliff and overlooking a vastness of water. All felt well, serene, at peace. And still, within that energy, an element of surrender, as I had my throat cut from behind and fell down toward the water. It sounds terrible, but in this vision it felt peaceful. I saw myself floating down like a feather, rather than violently, I landed on the water and was received into her depths, cocooned, as if all that had come before that moment was cleansed and transmuted.

On further exploration, this was a mercy killing by my daughter. This has me exploring the concept that within my lineage there has to be an element of hurt to set the next generation free. This is something I am still sitting with though.

Where there is hurt, there can be healing. Here is another past life I have extensively worked with.

Calvan- 'Little Bald One'

I was a Biblical scribe called Calvan, and, funnily enough, was a little man with a balding head! I spent years writing scripture by candlelight. Devoted to God and the church (me - I know, right!). I took a vow before

God to be humble, to only receive what I needed, to have basic sustenance and a simple existence. That vow was binding, not just in that lifetime, but to carry forward. In remembering and healing this past life, I unlocked the memory of the skillsets I had then and have brought forward now, but also soul contracts and vows. I released Calvan from his vow of a basic existence in devotion to God, giving reassurance that in his lifetime he was true to this, but that vow is no longer needed here in this lifetime I am living. That my Soul be released from that vow, so I can henceforth and not be bound by a basic existence. That I am worthy and deserving to receive more than the bare minimum. But also, with the knowledge that this past life has brought forward positives - the ability to embody devotion, patience, gratitude, and the gift of writing.

'Shifu' ("Shee - Foo") - Master (worker). To teach or coach, often associated with martial arts teachers.

This is the one of my past lives that I am most reluctant to explore, because it is linked to a phobia of mine, and so the thought of going deeper in to explore gives me 'the fear' (literally!). But I know just enough to begin to understand why I have this phobia and where it came from.

What is this phobia? Pandas. Yes, the black and white bears. My earliest memory of this really bothering me is around the age of 10 and onwards. I remember looking through an animal encyclopaedia at school and coming across a page with a vicious looking, teeth-bearing panda, and this must've sparked the past life remembrance for me, because since then I've been petrified.

On several occasions I have braved it to journey into this past life, bit by bit, because it feels terrifying, but I wanted answers. Which leads me to introducing 'Shifu', a little boy, around age 6-8, living among the Chinese rainforest with his family. His father was a protector of the community. I haven't been shown much of that past life apart from the 'final day'. I was wandering/playing in the forest, gathering sticks and interesting bits I found, and I strayed away from the marked path. I lost awareness of what was around me as I ventured further in among the trees and bamboo *(I am literally feeling a fear-sweat and panic setting in as I describe this!)* and I heard a rustle ahead. Looking up, there it was, the black and white fur, with big black eyes staring into my soul. I dropped everything and ran. I felt like I was running forever, and then I fell through the forest floor down into a deep man-made ditch and was impaled on carved bamboo spikes.

It wasn't the panda that killed me, but that fear by association remains. The horror and panic and then that being the last experience before my death. This is a prime example of how our past lives can manifest as fears, and physical and emotional symptoms in our current life time. There is probably more that I could discover about this past life, and will very likely go in to do some conscious past life healing, but right now, I think I'll wait!

This reiterates that we can carry so much into our current lifetime from past lives - good and not so good. Should we choose to do the work, to discover and even heal past life trauma, this can positively impact us tenfold! Perhaps finding forgiveness, recognising skill, voiding or fulfilling soul contracts, becoming aware of how past lives may have manifested in this lifetime and moving forward, free from chains, with inspiration or at its simplest - a sense of fulfilment or release!

I'm sure I could write a book alone on past lives, ones that I have explored and past lives as a topic in general. But these are the lives that have impacted me the most so far and the ones I have been called deeper to explore, it would seem for specific reasons. I genuinely believe, albeit some may say that I'm wrong, but that in past life discovery and exploration, we likely do not receive all at once. We unlock each one that needs conscious acknowledgement at the time, which bears lessons, skills, experiences or patterns that are to be looked at, retrieved or broken, to call in healing and closure, for deeper understanding of our current self, or any other reason that life may be relevant to the time it is discovered.

But how can a past life affect you now, here in this current life? If my own personal examples haven't given enough insight or explanation, we can learn, gain and release much from past lives. An injury, fatal or not, from a past life can manifest in this lifetime as an illness, a pain, a mark on the body. A hurt or betrayal can manifest into those feelings being carried forward into this lifetime, often otherwise inexplicable, especially any fears and phobias.

There is so much to be said from past lives. They are a window to our past that can shed light on our present. And so, I'd love to gift you the opportunity to journey to one of your own past lives through guided meditation. This is another gift from me to you.

You can use this meditation as many times as you like, to revisit the same past life, or to explore different ones. I would welcome you to set the intention to connect with the past life most relevant to what is needed, or rising in you, right now. This is a guide - you are welcome to set your own specific intention, either way. I would recommend you take some time to get clear on your desired outcome before tuning in.

Past Life Meditation Link: -
https://anuveya.mysite.app/pastlife

Enter the code BOOK to get free access to the audio.

After the meditation, I would strongly advise you to journal and note down your experience, even the parts that don't seem to make sense. You can always revisit at a later date with a clearer or more informed mind.

Mini Epilogue:- It is important to note that, while we can uncover all of these wounds and acknowledge, work through and hopefully heal from, there is no pinnacle 'healed self'. No finish line where you get to brush your hands off and say "Okay, I've done it!". As you meander through life, uplevelling, experiencing new things and uncovering more information, you will find that more wounds or parts of the shadow self will become apparent. It's not a linear 'here to there' journey, but one that keeps us constantly evolving. The trick is not to become complacent in moving through it for fear of what comes next, but to be open to and aware of the fact that we will be thrown curveballs and hurdles to overcome what we need to in order to reach our next level selves, and that each level comes with a new "boss" to defeat.

The Women

This was a hard pill to swallow for me. Before I go any deeper, I want to say that, rather than giving advice on how to work through and release your own wounds, I'll be sharing my own experience, and that anything within this chapter is subjective. Take what resonates and leave what doesn't. We all feel, hurt, heal and experience differently.

Throughout this book so far, I've been open and transparent, and intend to continue doing so. However, I won't lie, there are parts of me feeling fear, deep vulnerability and the urge to run and hide under a cosy blanket instead of writing this chapter. At the same time, I am feeling completely liberated, and like I finally have a voice worthy of being heard.

I've spoken candidly about many of my experiences so far in this book, but another factor that weighs heavily, is mine but not mine at the same time.

For generations, there has been a recurring pattern in my family that mothers and daughters have a strained relationship. I'm not so sure about my great-great grandmother, but for the past 4 generations, this has been a cycle that has been quite prolific. And so, it feels like I'm the one that bears the responsibility to break the chain, to free my lineage from this pattern, and to release our female line from whatever this is.

Each woman in my family is or was a very forward, strong willed woman. From my Great Grandmother (affectionately known as Granny Pops) to my grandma, my mum, my sister and myself.

I'm probably the one that is the most mellow, withheld and doesn't just 'say it how it is' regardless of what anyone thinks, says or does. To be honest, I'm probably the one who was most complacent, eager to please and able to keep my mouth shut. Which is maybe why I'm having a very different experience to the others, and why I'm not only more conscious of this pattern, but also actively trying to break free from it.

These women in my family have historically, and in modern times, been in relationships and marriages with military men. This is another pattern, but one I have broken free from. I have the utmost respect for each of them, but living a life secondary to a soldier and his work was not only something that never spoke to me, but it was a lifestyle I grew up in, and didn't want that for my own children. In being a military partner, there is that element of losing who you are or putting her on the back burner, and perhaps that is an element of why this pattern persists? Women who were girls with big hopes and dreams, who instead settled for safety and security, living a life where their dreams became a distant memory. Did this fuel the angst between them all? The want for their daughter to be more, the want to not turn out like their mother, the desire to prove the last generation wrong? Or perhaps a hidden and unspoken jealousy that each of the daughters was a step closer to breaking free.

Is there this subconsciously irresistible cog that turns within each of us, that puts a pressure onto the generation that follows? To question them, to judge, even ridicule them? To make them question their worth, their ability, and the capability to be a woman in the eyes of the women before her? I have often felt the weight and pressure of feeling disapproval. That my way isn't the 'done' way, or the questioning of why I have or haven't done a specific thing. For so long, I would fret over the worry of being a disappointment, or being judged and questioned, for sometimes what seemed like no reason. But now I'm my own person and, although there are still elements of being questioned and probably judged, I have both made it known and reinforced my boundaries that it doesn't affect me, at least not even nearly as much as it used to.

I can't speak for the other women in my family, to how they feel and think, but I can say with certainty that I know that I am different. That I am different from them, but also different in the grand scheme of things too. That I have come here with a mission to break this chain. Not just to free myself and my ancestors, but to free my lineage, my own children and to open up a new pathway forward.

Ancestral healing has been a big part of my spiritual journey, and it continues to be. I've been stuck between this rock and a hard place of seeing these patterns recurring, but also being a pattern of my own, probably more difficult than that of a really crappy or non-existent relationship. My relationship with my own mother has been a real mixed bag, and to be really honest, difficult to write about. Not because our relationship is awful, but because there seems to be a constant push and pull. That feeling as though I'm caught between feeling like we are best friends one moment, and then at another, I am unable to please her. No matter how hard I try, or even when I don't try, there's the echo of displeasure in what I am or am not doing. A feeling of not measuring up to invisible standards or being questioned about something that I have or haven't done. I understand that this is probably coming from a place of love and best intention, but more often than not, I can't help but feel like I'm just being ground down. For the past few years, I'd come to the conclusion that there was going to be something or other, regardless of what I did, so I decided that I would do what I wanted, and any opinions or comments cast upon me were secondary and more or less irrelevant. Since then, not only have I felt a big shift in my anxiety and mental health, but also, I have been making choices more aligned with who I am, not what people want me to be.

During the majority of retreats or workshops I've either joined or facilitated, one of my main intentions has been to shift this 'mother weight' and heal my lineage, for myself and for the others before and after me. For a long time though, I felt like it was all about me. Not in a self-centred way, but like I was the victim, the one in receipt of the unnecessary comments. But through the work I have done on myself, teamed with my own experience of being a mother, I know that it's not all about me. Even at time when my mum may have said something that made me feel like a piece of crap, or made a remark that was clearly a passive aggressive way of getting her point across, it wasn't because of me or anything I had or hadn't done, but because my mother has her own battles to face, many of which I likely know nothing about and probably never will. The times when she had spoken to me in a short tone of voice, I'd spend ages agonising over what I'd done wrong. However, from personal motherhood experience, I get that she may have been dealing with something stressful and upsetting, or perhaps just feeling overwhelmed and unappreciated.

That said, I came into this chapter with the preconception of writing about a turbulent relationship that was one-sided and, from my point of view, has been a focus of worry and lack of self-worth for years. To my mum, it's just a normal relationship with her daughter, oblivious to any turbulence felt from my side. But as I write, I know that I have seemed to have developed a whole different perspective, and I am a little further down the path of my healing journey.

Instead, I now want to write about understanding, compassion and knowing that even if something is directed towards you, it's not always about you. Rather than just detaching from these people mentally, emotionally, physically or spiritually, it's about gaining perspective, and also seeing that there is always a lesson. It seems for me that this lesson is to see the bigger picture. To not just focus on myself and my own healing, but to embrace the fact that, yes, the ancestral healing does fall on my shoulders. To heal myself, I must also heal the lineage - not just cutting myself away from it and breaking free from a chain, but instead to forge that chain in strength, and become a stronger link for the next generation, while showing appreciation and understanding to the women who came before me. They are the ones who have suffered, as well as I. Each of us, a personal suffering to add to the chain, but in turn, generational experience, wisdom and resilience.

A pivotal moment for me recently was when I attended a glorious Goddess Festival at a fantastic venue in Dorset. I was guided through a 'Tree of Life' meditation, where I was shown 'twisted roots', where my roots were entwined with others' roots, and so I was being restricted. Within this meditation, I was gifted a pink diamond, and received the strength to cut those roots, detaching and untangling myself. I then moved onto a goddess dance workshop - totally up my street! I fully immersed myself in the flow of my movement and rhythm. I could feel the energy and healing codes flowing through my entire being. I felt liberated and free.

Towards the end of the festival, we gathered around a fire, chanting, singing, and drumming. It was a beautiful ceremony, celebrating the group of women that had come together to share the day. To close the ceremony, we were invited to shout the name of a woman from our lineage into the fire, to support healing in whichever way was needed. On three, I shouted my Mum's name and immediately felt a wave of emotion come over me. I felt goosebumps all over and I was moved to tears. At first, I felt guilt, like I was throwing my own mother into the fire, but I quickly realised it wasn't that at all. The emotions I was feeling weren't sadness and pain; it was relief. As if anything that was bearing weight on my mother's Soul was burned and released. Cutting cords for her, instead of directly for me. I felt an echo of energy, so deep as if it echoed through me and my lineage, blowing out and ancestral cobwebs that have been stowing away. Since then, I've felt such a shift, with feelings of freedom, heightened creativity, being able to pursue my dreams, and seeing it generate returns, tenfold!

So, what I've learned here? Although I will continue on with pursuing healing for my ancestry, it is knowing that to free ourselves, sometimes we have to free others. To generate opportunity for them to clear their path, or if we are able to, to maybe clear a little bit for them. When less weight is bearing down on them, less weight is bearing down on us. This doesn't mean to actively step in for them and do the work on their behalf. It's knowing that even something as simple (although difficult) as showing understanding, or willingness to see from a different perspective so that we may have a better idea of what is not about us but about them. In turn taking the heaviness, guilt, shame, resentment, and anxiety away from who we are, or are not, and knowing that anything that has made us feel that way is a projection and result of their own hurt.

We are not responsible for their healing, but in finding understanding, it can support us in our own healing.

Mini Epilogue:- Throughout this chapter I have focused backwards, because exploring my ancestral lineage and healing the patterns within were a priority; knowing I could break the chain and clear the way. Now I'm at a point where, since this chapter was written, much has transpired which has pivoted my views, bringing me into a space and mindset where I actually feel at ease with all that I have mentioned. I can stand in the knowing that I have broken the chain for my personal downline, and healed what I can so far. In a way that feels positive for me, where I can experience more nourishing connections with the women in my family, but maintain my own autonomy and boundaries. So my focus is now drawn to what, and more so who, comes next. As much as we can look back and recognise and break patterns for ourselves, we must remember that we are clearing the way forward. Not in a way that shields and restricts, but in a way that offers more opportunity, perhaps opportunity we, or those before us never had. It also brings me into reflection of how I am as a mother, the impact I'm having on our next generation, and to make sure that any patterns I have tried so hard to break do stop with me. I have to say that you, nor I, will ever be the perfect mother, but we can be a more conscious mother and that alone is a gift in itself to our next generation. Whether you have young children, adult children, or no children, it will positively influence the way we interact and react to the younger people in our lives. We can break the chain from the past, but we must remember to leave a legacy that will honour our work and efforts for their future.

All Hail the Golden Child

It is a recurring joke in my family that I am the 'Golden Child'. In my opinion, this is not because I'm the favourite, but more so because I am the 'best behaved'. No discredit to my siblings, but I was usually the good girl, the one that caused least fuss, did as she was told, did relatively well in school and barely asked for much, if anything. That said, the joke prevails, and there always seems to be a presumption of favouritism towards me, although that's not the case.

Being dubbed the Golden Child isn't all it's cracked up to be. In fact, it's been more of a burden than a blessing. Besides it contributing to any sibling rivalry, it's also contributed heavily to me being too submissive, complacent and self-sabotaging. As we all know by this point, I am a prolific people pleaser, afraid to rock the boat, bring unwanted attention, rejection or punishment to myself. So, I'd often choose the 'good' route. The one that'll keep me in the good books, causing less of a fuss, and (hopeful) to receive the praise and acknowledgement I craved. This was usually to my detriment. I withheld things I wanted to express; I resisted things I wanted to do - for fear of displeasing others.

Many recognise the struggles of the family 'black sheep', thinking that the golden child always gets it easy. In fact, being the golden child is not easy at all!

We are the ones that are seen as 'okay', so we apparently don't require as much support, attention or guidance. We can either be self-sufficient or need less input. However, that transpires to us having less of what we actually need. Time and energy are diverted towards those who are the tearaways and the black sheep, the ones who apparently need to be saved. The golden child is okay, right!? They're doing well, they always manage, and they're so good that they don't need any help! In turn, we develop coping mechanisms to accommodate that.

The number of times I wanted to scream at people, smash something, to do something completely ridiculous, or to cause a scene. But instead, I held any frustration internally, not causing a fuss. Not giving people reason to talk about me in a negative way. I (mostly) did as I was told. I paid attention in school, I worked hard. I helped to look after my siblings when my mum was ill and my dad was away. I was good at things, things that my parents could brag about to others. I was great at art and anything creative. I taught myself to play the keyboard by sound matching. My mum proudly volunteered me to play *"Right Here Waiting"* by Richard Marx to any visitors we had. I went to college. I had goals and ambitions. I was accepted into university (albeit I later dropped out). I was independent. I have two amazing children, a happy home and a good partner. I passed my driving test. I've had/have nice cars. I live in a lovely village. I have a successful business. Life is pretty good, and so from a bragging perspective, my family has a lot to brag about.

But what happens when shit hits the fan?

If I need help, if I've done something I shouldn't, or that won't be approved off…I have become much more resilient and self-sufficient. Equally, I often fall into the mindset of dealing with things myself, either so nobody finds out, or to maintain my squeaky-clean persona. But I've gone through stages of self-destruction, when I've done things I'm not proud of, merely for an opportunity to be a bad girl, to go against the grain, and to feel the rush of adrenaline that comes from taking risks. In recent years, it's been less self-destruct and more self-discovery. Operating from a place of curiosity, of wanting to really explore who I am, what I do and don't like. Taking opportunities where, not only can I meet myself, but to express myself, to feed my cravings and to experience life from the perspective of a woman more in alignment of who she is. There will always be a part of me deep inside that still holds that fearful, people pleasing nature, but I have grown to become a version of myself that is so confident in who she is that it's undisputable. To be myself on a level that, even if it doesn't fit with others' expectations, that I am being authentic.

This way, it does a few things. First of all, it will filter out those who depend on me for what I can do for them, or those who only want a watered down, complacent version of me. Then, it shows people who I really am, affirming my place in society, setting an expectation on my own terms. It will also welcome in, attract and cement the connections with the people who are both meant to be in my life, and also who respect and love me for me.

As a younger child, the whole 'Golden Child' thing didn't really seem relevant, as I always felt my sister and I were treated equally. Looking back, I did have a very strong bond with my Mum, but in hindsight, that's likely the old soul in me that was more capable of making strong adult connections. It was more so when my brother, 11 years younger than me, was born. I doted on him entirely. He was the apple of my eye, and at the age of 11-12, I had this newfound sense of responsibility. Being dependable and protective. From there it fed this golden child persona - the one that was the helper and did good. Into my teens, I was mostly away during the week at boarding school, and then moved away for college. During this time, my sister and I had gone in totally separate directions. I was the 'do-gooder' and she was the rebel. The contrast between us only enhanced the Golden Child label for me, highlighting how 'in line' I actually was. This created a rift between us both as I was perceived as the favourite, although it wasn't true - we all know that my brother is the favourite! (For reference, the favourite and the golden child, especially in this context, are definitely not the same!)

Into my late teens and early 20's, where I did find my rebellious streak, I still felt that pressure of the golden child looming over me. To not be too much of anything, but with the crippling fear of not being enough. That feeling of being trapped between a rock and a hard place. I mostly made decisions based on what others would think, especially if my family would approve. I opted to do things in the hopes of acknowledgement and the metaphorical pat on the head for being a good, clever girl. But then for a while, that ache to not feel boxed in or to be slapped with the good girl label meant I did become rebellious. That didn't serve me well at all. But in the grand scheme of things, I was never a bad girl. I have never been in trouble with the police or done anything so awful that it's caused a massive rift. It was a more self-destructive rebellion. The kind of rebellion that likely caused embarrassment and likely more so, because I 'want that type of girl'. Back then, I didn't care what they thought because I was in a bad place and just genuinely didn't really care about anything.

Now I don't really care what they think because I know my own mind. I have my own life, values and beliefs, but there is still that little voice in my head, the one I try my hardest not to listen to, probing and nudging at me to keep in line, to be the good girl, live up to expectations, not to disappoint, and to uphold the persona. I used to let that voice win more often than not, but what happened there was that I wasn't choosing me - I was choosing the version of me that I thought I had to and the version that I thought others wanted me to be. This led me down many paths that turned out to be dead ends, feeling like I was really getting somewhere, while receiving the cheering on and acknowledgement I craved. This turned out to only lead me to a version of myself that wasn't really me.

Now, it's still a long-standing family joke that I'm the Golden Child, but that's all it is: a joke. It's something we giggle about, not a persona I feel I must live up to. And I'm glad, because the proof is in the pudding. When I do follow my own heart and mind, I end up exactly where I'm supposed to be, with an abundance of opportunities that seem to effortlessly flow. When I do so, the Universe is cheering me on with arms in the air, while watching me merrily on my way, smashing my personal goals, living my dreams and experiencing the world in the way that I was always meant to.

Just because the grass appears to be greener, it doesn't mean it is better! The grass is probably greener, because everyone has spent so much time trawling through the metaphorical allotment of those who appear to need it. The golden child's green has thrived mostly through being left alone. It's become wild, like these places where, due to lack of human interaction, have thrived to create its own ecosystem. It is a thing of beauty from first glance, but among that beauty is chaos, tangled roots, undergrowth riddled with junk, and a complex system entrenched in parasites. But from the outside, I guess it looks fine.

Just because someone is dubbed the Golden Child, the favourite, or any other title that indicates that they have been put on a pedestal - please don't judge that they have it all. I mean, it's lovely that I'm seen as being so 'awesome', but equally, there are times when I've really needed more help than I've let on, with stories left untold and problems that have had to be solved alone.

Mini Epilogue:- How to adult when you've been/are the golden child... The concept of 're-parenting' has since come to my attention. That doesn't mean that we were necessarily parented in a bad way, or that we've been parented wrong, but it means to parent your inner child in a way that nourishes what they need/needed, and to give yourself the opportunity and attention as an adult that the little you could have really used. Recognising yourself as an individual, with individual needs and skills. To create and facilitate space for you to be, explore and feel what the younger you should have. Now that doesn't mean start playing with dolls, or get the Lego out (Unless that's what you want to do!), but to generate the emotions and experience that you required from doing those things. Perhaps Little You was craving to be acknowledged, heard and seen. Or maybe you wanted to move more; dance, jump, run. Or maybe you wanted to get messy, paint, play in the mud, bake. It's not just in the doing either, but also in the feeling, allowing yourself to feel and express yourself in ways that feel safe to you, where you may have held yourself back or been restricted. If you parented yourself in a way that was what you needed, how would that look?

Spirit Guides & Higher Power

Meditation IS a window to the Soul! It's a portal to another dimension and a journey to our deepest and highest depths.

Despite my experience as a psychic medium, my true spiritual journey only really began when I found meditation and journalling. It seems basic and often comes with a preconception of what those things are.

Meditation is sitting cross-legged under a tree, finger and thumb together, and making a humming sound, right? You'll be surprised how common that stereotype comes up! But meditation is what you make it. It is a powerful tool and a window into much more than you can begin to imagine. Personally, meditation was my starting place to connect deeper, not just with myself, but with my guides and external energies, to receive clarity, confirmation, inspiration and more. But to begin with I entered my practice with fear - fear that I would do it wrong, fear of what I would tune in to and receive, and fear of the unknown. Despite what some may say, there is no wrong way to meditate. The best way that works for you is the right way.

It could be sitting upright on a mat or cushion, with your hand placed specifically, in silence or with soft music. It could be during dance or movement, where you get lost in your own energy and everything else melts away. It could be walking through your favourite place. It could be listening to music, running, cooking, painting - whatever your safe space is. The place that you feel you can get lost in yourself but become so beautifully found, all at the same time. What matters is not the posture and circumstance, but the intention, how you feel and creating sacred space for yourself to delve in and openly receive. So don't let the fear of failure or the unknown hold you back from giving it a go. Don't let specifics stop you from trying.

I have received the most profound information while in meditation. I have uncovered the deepest parts of myself, connected with guides, received healing, inspiration and divine connection. Meditation also acts as a workout for the third eye and your intuition. You may not see or experience much to begin with but, with time and practice, you will develop. Seeing and feeling more. Even if being a psychic medium is your goal, here you can refine what and how you receive, strengthening your ability and skills.

How do you know it's not just nonsense?

How do you keep track of it?

Where do you seek/receive validation?

This is where journalling comes in. Had you asked me years ago what my take on what journalling was, I'd have assumed you meant in terms of a teenage girl, affectionately writing her thoughts, trials and tribulations in a diary. This is important in itself, but now, when I talk about journalling, it's more than a recording or pouring your heart out. It's a sacred book of your Soul's experiences, where you can journal your dreams, intentions, experiences. Where you can channel divine information, letting the pages become filled with sacred scripture, soulful words and imagery. Where you can record your meditation, sacred journeys, self-practice, collective experiences and more. Where you can note down any information you receive, always dating it, and looking back at a later date, receiving validation that the information you received was correct, even if you didn't trust it at the time, or opening a page at random to read channelled words that really hit the spot right at the moment you need them. Journalling also serves as a point of contemplation, in the times when you don't know, or when you want to dig deeper. Having specific questions to journal on can be immensely helpful, whether they are general questions to regularly journal on, or specific to a certain aspect.

This may be new to you, or you may be well seasoned in meditation and journalling, so step into this at your own angle. Here are some journalling prompts to meditate on and work with, if you feel called to.

Journalling Prompts: -

- Where am I experiencing blockages or lack?

- How is this influencing my current self?

- What do I need to release or build on?

- How will my life look and feel when I am no longer experiencing blocks or lack?

- What is the first/next step I can take in achieving this?

Do not panic, you will feel like you don't know. You will feel like you don't have the answers, and then your ego will kick in to overdrive and either try to answer these questions for you, or you will feel a state of not-knowing. This is normal. That is why it is important to go deeper and to go within. To really connect with yourself, letting go of ego, letting go of the need to do/think/say a certain way. Surrender yourself and truly sink in, becoming open with yourself and ready to listen.

You may see visually. You may hear, feel, or sense. Whichever way you connect to yourself is fine as long as you're getting something. It doesn't even need to make sense. This is why journalling is so helpful, because you can document it in the moment and then look back, sitting with it, or perhaps doing some research. For example, you may not receive a profound and definitive answer, but maybe you see a blue flower, or hear the sound of a particular animal. In this day and age, the internet is a great and useful tool, as well as books, if you have them, but with the infinite information online, you can look up the meaning in a matter of minute and then interpret from there. So just know that you don't have to gain all of the answers, but at least be open to receiving them, in various forms, whether they come or not. And above all, trust! Trust in yourself, your intuition, and your skill. Trust it all and know that what is meant to come through, will. If you don't get a full answer, follow the breadcrumbs in the meantime.

It was through my own personal journey with meditation and visualisation that I connected and continue to connect with my spirit guides and higher energetic beings. As it stands, I currently have 8 guides I consciously work with, either individually or all at once. Calling them in for protection and guidance. When I hold and facilitate space for others, offering healing and a safe space, I call in all of my guides. I see them visually but feel them energetically. Always standing in the same order - the order that I connected with them on a conscious level. I visualise them stood with me in circle, each guide in turn gifting me an 'orb' of coloured energy. Let me introduce you to my guides:

Guide One - Kalandhi - *"The sun, bringer of light"*

Very Theravada Buddhist monk-like in appearance. Elderly with a bald head, but with a long tuft of grey beard and quite long earlobes. He wears an orange 'kasaya' (traditional robe). He is beautifully serene and has such peaceful energy, with an unspoken feeling of unconditional protection. His presence supports me to feel at ease, knowing I am safe and not alone.

Kalandhi was the first guide to come to me. This was during my mediumship work. He was, and is, my gatekeeper, ensuring only spirit and energies with the best intention come through. During my mediumship work, I'd visualise him like my lovely little bodyguard, keeping watch over my waiting room of spirits, all eager to squeeze in and come through during readings.

Guide Two - Tulah - my wise protector - *"Balance"*

Tulah came to me as I was nearing the end of my mediumship work. I was exhausted, energetically and spiritually drained, and was working a lot with spirit and other energies. I really needed to up my spiritual security, and in came Tulah; a force to be reckoned with. In appearance, I always describe him as 'Gandalf-like', because he is a HUGE man and is easily 9ft tall. He has grey hair and a long grey beard, is very pale blue in aura, is dressed in a long grey-blue cloak, and always carries a tall wooden staff with a wispy blue orb on the top. He is a force to be reckoned with, yet I can feel his kind soft nature. Tulah supports me with protection, and often acts as a guiding light within times of darkness.

When I work with Tulah, he gifts me a small, yet powerful orb of wispy blue light. I feel this move around within my hands, almost dancing, encouraging my hands to channel and receive healing codes, before it is either received by myself, or passed on to those receiving healing.

Guide Three - Tanka - "*Grounding, healing and wisdom*"

(In Lakota spirituality, 'Wakan Tanka' is the term for the sacred or the divine. Often translated as the "Great Spirit" and can be interpreted as the power or the sacredness that resides in everything, so I feel incredibly blessed to have Tanka as one of my guides.)

When I first connected with Tanka, I was slightly resistant, not because she felt scary or bad, but because I had this fear of playing into a stereotype, that it was 'too cliché' to have a Native American spirit guide. I questioned if this was a real connection or just my mind playing into an ideal of what spirit guides 'should' be like. Through surrendering and opening myself up to connect deeper with her, I found such a profound and deep connection and the story of who she is and was. I witnessed her in two forms. One of these forms is a shaman, an elderly medicine woman, with a wrinkled face, evidently blessed with wisdom. At first, she appeared to hold the aesthetic of a frail old woman, but when you look into her eyes, you see the power she holds within - humble yet strong. I have also witnessed her in her younger years as a huntress with a heart for adventure, a love of exploring nature, a zest for life, and the strength of a warrior. I was gifted incredible channelled imagery of her riding horseback across the planes under a beautiful sunset, with the wind in her hair and a feeling of solace and escape.

Tanka brings to me much healing - physically, emotionally, and spiritually - but also deep wisdom. The energy she gives is so potent, very earthy, and grounded, yet otherworldly. When she gifts me her energy, it is received in the form of a large deep earthy red light. It is rocklike but weightless, though the sheer energy requires my whole palms to receive and pass on when healing.

Guide Four - Nukitru - *"Femininity, love and self-care"*

Nukitru brings a welcome softness to my spirit team. Her energy can only be described like being surrounded by butterflies, with a sense of wonder, awe and beauty. Her energy is powerfully serene. She is a woman standing in her power, unapologetically, full of unconditional love and respect for herself. She emanates divine feminine energy. She has beautiful dark skin, long braided dark hair, with strands of blue and red, is adorned with sky-blue painted markings on her face, gold jewellery, and draped in a soft pink over-the-shoulder robe. She is power and grace combined. Nukitru supports me in coming back into my softness, to know it is safe to be. When I feel vulnerable or manically operating from a space of wounded masculine, she gently guides me back into alignment and balance.

When she gifts me her energy, it is like a soft pink power of light, enabling me to move it in my hands to receive the codes, but then to softly 'blow' or sprinkle the energy out to those receiving it, like a magickal healing dust.

Guide Five - Attayah - *"Star seed connection, protection, power"*

Attayah, to me, feels and looks like a female energy, but 'she' is almost androgynous. An otherworldly, star seed image, with pale blue, almost white, skin, long white hair, an electric blue glow swept back away from her face, and big dark glossy eyes. She is tall and slender. She wears light blue fabrics wrapped around and draped over her, and carries a bow and tube of arrows - arrows with double arrowpoints on them. From my deeper connection with Attayah and research, I have come to learn that she is from Andromedan origin.

> *"Andromedans are Beings of Light who are dedicated to bringing new technologies and holistic forms of healing to the whole Universe. They also strive to assist other star-nations to live in peace and unity. "*– 'Andromeda, Pleiades, Sirius, Star Seed Guide' by Eva Marquez

Attayah is my guide for protection, strength and connection to the higher realms. She is a soul guardian. She comes full of love but has a sternness to her. She says very little but communicates strongly through energy and making facial gestures. When I work with Attayah, I am gifted a blue light of energy, which glides within my hands before being pulled back, as if an arrow within a bow, and catapulted forward, delivering the healing energy to be received.

Guide Six - Qasid ('Kah-seed') - *"Messenger/courier, intention, a path that is smooth".*

Now this guy is one jolly dude! Always a smile, and with a BIG energy. Appearance-wise, he looks like a stereotypical genie with a mostly bald head, a black ponytail, pointed eyebrows, and a thin draping moustache. He has muscular arms, but a rounded belly. He is topless, with gold hareem-like trousers that fade into a golden wisp - though there is definitely no genie lamp! He has such a big energy, so full and present.

Qasid is my abundance guide. Not just money, but abundance in all areas - love, opportunity, health and more. He supports me to manifest and bring in what I need, and to be more open to receiving in full flow, even if I don't know that I need it at that time. When I work with Qasid, I am gifted a golden glowing light energy, like gold dust, which is then sprinkled and blown out to be received.

Guide Seven - Nagini ('Nah-jee-nee') - *"Goddess Parvati. Almost perfect. A female that turns into a large snake. Shakti energy"*

A beautifully powerful guide, I am yet to work with - in the way she is intended. I think this is more so on my part. There is certainly internal resistance deep within, though I know she is a force to be reckoned with and has already led me through some tough lessons, so I am definitely willing to go further with her.

Nagini has an ancient beauty to her, tanned skin, straight dark hair, and a curvaceous yet muscular figure. She is draped in fabric around the waist, her breasts are adorned with golden paint, and she wears a combination of gold and turquoise jewellery. She holds her hands out, one with a ball of fire, the other with golden scales. Her name alone indicates a connection with the snake. Along with the golden snake armband, she completely embodies the Shakti/Kundalini energy, and I'm sure she is here to guide me to do the same. Nagini beckons me to go deep within myself in many aspects, to explore my deepest wounds, from this lifetime and past lifetimes, and to re-evaluate the narratives that have formed and shaped my realities. She invites me to check my connection with myself, and others around me.

I know she is here to support me in moving through a lot of powerful stuff. Though I say 'support', it often feels like a hard push, but I know it is for my highest good. As well as the deep healing and discovery that there is to be done, Nagini is also here to empower me further with my womanhood, enhancing my Sacral energy and connection - creatively, sensually, and in nourishing my own needs. To stand in my power, stronger, firmer, with a roaring fire in my belly, so I can grasp life with both hands and live it the way I am meant to.

When I work with Nagini, she comes with a flame-like aura around her with a blue inner core, then fading out into the fiery orange. The energy she gives me is like a ball of fire. I can feel the heat in my hands as I receive her healing codes then, like beautifully poetic fireworks, they disperse and rain down, before I push the energy forward towards those receiving.

Guide Eight - Irfan (The Fox) - *"Knowledge, awareness, learning and wisdom".*

This spritely little guy is a bushy tailed, fluffy fox with a cheeky, playful energy. When I connect with him, he pounces around above my head, swishing his tail. He seems to jump, float and glide through the air. I very rarely see him on the actual ground. For years I've always resonated with the fox, and when I led an animal spirit guide meditation, this was when I first connected with Irfan. I always feel uplifted with him. His energy is like a soothing balm for me when I'm feeling anxious, heavy or in pain. He is definitely a comfort for me, but also supports me with his unspoken wisdom and knowing.

When I work with Irfan, I receive a green-teal colour glow. They look like small water droplets, making small ripples around my head and shoulders. I always feel the need to sway and move in a playful way when I work with his energy.

I always feel a bit greedy at the fact that I consciously and so strongly work with 8 guides, but they each have their own purpose individually, and I trust that it is the way it is meant to be. Collectively, they are a powerhouse for healing, which is why I always work with them when I'm healing. Of course, I call in the guides of those I work with, but I always have my own team supporting me and working with me, each one giving me their healing codes to pass on.

The way your guides come to you will depend on how you receive them, how you feel their presence, how they 'look', and also how you can connect and resonate most with them. Personally, I am very visual, so I see them, each one in human (or animal) form, but also with their associated colours. You may not see your guide, but you may feel them, hear them, just know their energy, equally, or they may not even appear as a recognisable being - perhaps as a colour, light, shape. There is no right or wrong. But either way, get to know them and form strong bonds with your team. When the bond is stronger, you will feel more confident in calling on them, working with them, and trusting them. You will also be able to recognise when they are sending signs and messages. This is how I learned the names of each of my guides - by making conscious connections and spending time with them, connecting in ways that felt most resonant with me. I like to journal on my guides and make sketches of them. When I receive their names, I love to do research into the meaning and origin of the name. More often than not, the information resonates with both what I have received, and also with the appearance, purpose and energy that they bring.

As well as guides, you may also experience connection with other higher energies, deities, gods/goddesses in their various forms, ascended masters, angels, nature spirits, and more. As with spirit guides, the more you work with them and get to know them, the stronger that connection will become. Some may be with you for a long time, while others will just be with you temporarily.

When you set your altar space, you can set the intention, as well as having visual icons or representations, and make specific offerings to them. This will bring you into a deeper connection with them, but also enhance your own personal practice.

Mini Epilogue:- In terms of what I can add here, I think I've already said most of it. My advice is to either set the intention or take up any experiences that will facilitate meeting and working with your guides. If you're already doing so, to deepen those connections, get to know them, get used to working with them, recognise their energy, how you receive them, and how you interact with them. The same goes for any angels, deities, etc. that you work with or feel drawn to. The best thing you can do is just explore. You can meditate or journal with them, equally you can do your own conscious research.

Sacred Places (Follow the Call)

What sacred places beckon you? Is there a place that emits a call to you, generating a strong yearning within you? Perhaps a feeling of remembrance, even though you haven't been there before? Or somewhere that when you are there, you feel completely at home, embraced in the surety that THIS is the place you are meant to be? Or maybe there is a place or area that you constantly come back to, even unintentionally. There are circumstances always mean that's where you end up.

There are a few places currently that 'whisper' to me, but not calling hard enough just yet, though I know I will get there some day. I'm sure I will share more about those places when the time comes, but currently, my personal sacred places, the ones that not only call to me and infuse me with a strong sense of remembrance, but also the places I also receive potent downloads, channellings and sacred energetic (and physical) initiations are the Scottish Highlands, especially Loch Ness, Glastonbury (Avalon), and my current home - Wiltshire.

I lived in Wiltshire when I was quite young, around age six to nine. At first, because my parents had split and it was just the place we moved to, we stayed a little while, and then, when my mum married my dad, we moved to an army quarter a few miles away, still in Wiltshire. I was still young and so I didn't feel a conscious pull to the land at that point, but now, in hindsight, that was where I lived during times that were either very transformative in terms of life as I knew it, or during phases of my life that shaped my future. Wiltshire held me during the challenging and transformative times, as I navigated and moved forward. Though we then moved to Germany, and Wiltshire became a distant memory for some time.

I was then beckoned back again, when, during the beginning of online chat rooms and social media sites like Bebo and MySpace became popular, and I reconnected with some of my school friends from Wiltshire. One of which, a primary school crush, turned into a long-distance, online relationship when I was 16. During the first few months, I came back to Wiltshire to stay with a friend not far from where he lived, so we got to see each other 'in real life', not just on a webcam. When I moved back to Northeast England for college, we would both travel to and fro, making the long journeys to see each other. Once again, Wiltshire called me back. During the time I was considering my university applications, I was planning to move back down to Wiltshire to be closer to him, but alas, the teenage first love turned to heartbreak and wasn't to be. Wiltshire became a no-go once again.

A few years passed again, and, as I've previously mentioned, I reconnected with another friend, which turned into a relationship. We made plans eventually for me to move to be with him…in Wiltshire, but that wasn't meant to be either.

It was like I was the fish swimming around and Wiltshire with the rod trying to catch me, every so often getting a bite, but never with the opportunity to fully reel me in. But it was through that friend that I met my Marc. Clearly the Universe pulled out all the stops with that one, as he was the hook that finally managed to catch me and reel me in. Since then, Wiltshire has not only become my home, but a place that I feel such a deep connection - to the land and to myself. A place where I conceived both of my children, where my daughter was born, and the place I am bringing them up. A beautiful place, where I'm in awe every day at the wonders this land offers, the rich history, the ley lines and sacred places (especially Avebury), as well as the breathtakingly magnificent landscape, where I am deeply grateful that this is where I have landed. It is a place that has held and homed me during many important moments of my life so far, a place that I feel I can call home - not an easy feat for a military child.

Another place I have always felt was the closest thing to home is the Scottish Highlands. My connection to the area has been there since birth, in this lifetime, but I most certainly have strong past life connections there too. With my family from Inverness, it's a place I spent much of my childhood, full of happy memories, and somewhere I regularly return to in adulthood too. But again, like a deep calling, I am always drawn to connect back with the land

and the energies there. Every time I feel so in awe at the landscape, where the air is fresher, the water cleaner, everything just more amplified. I feel like I really come alive, that my Soul feels like it's home. I love the area as a whole, but the place that calls to me the most is Loch Ness. I love the mystery, the vastness, the way the trees cascade on the tall hills and cliffs either side. The downward view, standing on Dores beach, looking down the horizon, along the water to where the hills seem to meet in the middle.

At Loch Ness, I always feel recharged, like I've been put back in my holster for a reboot of energy. But it's also one of the places I receive potent downloads. On the 2022 retreat I hosted in Inverness, I channelled and wrote the first part to my *'Thistle & Flame'* activation (the second part, channelled and written in Glastonbury.) It was also on that same retreat we visited Clava Cairns - a Bronze age cemetery, also known for one of the sites where the *Outlander* TV programme was filmed. While exploring the site, I immediately felt a strong, powerful energy, as did the other ladies with me. I could see and feel codes beaming down onto one of the cairns - which one of the others said she did too. I wanted to treat this space with sacred reverence, being mindful of the site's history and energy. I felt so strongly repelled by the trees on the right-hand side, with a physical pain in my neck and deep sense of sorrow, so I avoided going near them. I felt a strong pull to the cairn on the far left of the site. Leaving my bag with my electricals in at the entrance to the cairn - it felt the right thing to do - I walked in and stood in the centre.

Arms stretched out level with my hips and with open palms, I closed my eyes. I felt transported to another time or dimension. I was an elder woman, wrapped in a cloak type cloth - the 'shrouded medicine woman' as I wrote in my journal. I received an initiation, being wrapped in a shroud like hers, being gifted 'keys and codes, and being opened up to what was given. I wrote the following in my journal immediately after the experience: *'Encased in mystery, shrouded by magick, the ancient secrets of the stones are protected. Only known by the way-bearers. She is wise, yet she is scorned. Hurt by a history of witch trials, and in hatred. The She are protectors, martyrs to the stones, and to the true code purposes in 'avil'(?). Be with us, be welcomed and initiated into the circle of the way-bearers, protectors of magick, and keepers of truths. Carry forth the power, and possess the secrets, but only in higher consciousness, for the human mind cannot digest, nor dissect. Carry forth, keeper of truths, take with you the power and be enshrouded by the way-bearers before you. She is watching, but she is waiting, use it wisely.'*

Once I'd journalled, I walked back over to our group, each of them looking at me with a collective concern on their faces. *"Are you okay?"* they asked. *"You look blue!"*. Each of them agreed in unison. Apparently, I looked a different colour, as if a blue glow on my skin. I felt great though, having just had an incredible experience and energetic initiation; I felt almost supercharged. They asked what happened in the cairn, as I was in there for 'so long'. Was I? It only felt like a few minutes, but they said it was more like 20 minutes. It was a truly remarkable experience! When we arrived back at the retreat house, I started to look further into my journalling, especially the word 'Avil', as I had no idea what it was or meant. My research led me to find its meaning to be associated with 'renewal', and also with St Teresa of Avila, who was linked to the Catholic reformation. My mind was blown! I was initiated as a way-bearer and 'keeper of codes', which later made perfect sense, as only months after, I channelled the Sacred Colour Codes for the Astro Colour Theory System that I created and have been continuously developing.

I cannot write a chapter about my sacred places without giving Glastonbury a worthy mention. My first experience of Glastonbury was on a gorgeous retreat led by Genevieve McGuiness during Autumn Equinox 2021. I find it incredible that only now in 2023, I feel such a strong connection and affiliation with the land, which I'm sure will only grow stronger. The retreat came to an end, and immediately after I had a hunger to go back again. I had the strong feeling and knowing that I HAD to host my own retreats here, but my underlying sister wound was kicking in - I couldn't 'copy' her and run retreats here too! But it was calling deep within my core and I knew I had to. I also had the reassurance from Genevieve to do what I was led to do. I am so grateful to her, not only for that weekend alone and the experience, but also the continued space that she held for me, our sacred 1-1 sessions on my personal SHE journey, and beautiful support and mentorship. Genevieve truly is a beautiful soul, I am ever thankful that we connected, as in doing so, I was also connected with other women who have been a big part of my journey since.

From that first retreat, I have visited many times, personally and I have held my own retreats there. A place that keeps on giving every time. A place where I feel like I can be completely me, without judgement, but also a place where I fit, where I don't feel like an outcast, where I can connect with my kind of people. It is also a place that entices me deeper into my connection with myself. Into a sacred remembrance of the person I was, I am, and am meant to be. Every time I visit, it stirs an echo within me to delve deeper, to learn more, to experience more, and to reclaim who I am. Already in this book, I have mentioned times and places where I have channelled and received in Glastonbury, including the second part of my *'Thistle and Flame'* activation, which was received and written in St Margaret's chapel. I adore Glastonbury, and I know that it has more to offer, by way of channellings, soul tribe connections, and deeper immersion into who I am.

My best recommendations to visit, if you get the opportunity to go are:

The Chalice Well & Gardens

The White Spring

St Margaret's Chapel & Magdalene Alms-houses

The Goddess Temple

As well as so many incredible shops to explore on the high street. It truly is a magickal place.

Mini Epilogue:- There are other places I am called to and yet to explore. But of the places I've already mentioned, those are the ones I return to time and time again. I can feel that I am being called further afield, and I know that deeper wisdom and experience is waiting for me. The next on my list are Cornwall, Wales and Ireland. There are sacred sites and places outside of the U.K. calling to me, and I know those nudges and opportunities will come in time. For now I really am energetically held within the British Isles, which actually does feel more resonant for me. I know I have other soul lineages from afar, but one of my most prominent lineages in this current lifetime, and previous, is the Celtic lineage, and one I want to explore deeper before embarking on exploring others.

She Who Is Birthed Through Fire

What does it mean - 'She who is birthed through fire'? It is a true baptism of fire, a birthing of you into your most aligned form, through a series of events and experiences that have shaped you up until this point. A metaphorical step through the ring of fire that could have burnt and destroyed you, but has made you. That said, I am a firm non-believer in the whole 'everything happens for a reason', but I do believe that those of us who have experienced such things are more equipped to take on the underbelly of the world, so that we may come out triumphant and be able to stand on top of the world with our head held high, knowing we have battled through such things and still reached a pinnacle point in our lives. She who is birthed through fire is intended to be a phrase of empowerment, a term that we have been forged and come out with an unfathomable strength and as a force to be reckoned with. A being of duality, for we have seen both the dark and the light, and with that acknowledgement, we venture forth without such a rose-tinted view of the world around us. We can be logical and subjective, but we can still be the dreamers and adventurers, for we already know that even through adversity, we can still be capable, to achieve our goals, to live our dreams, and to bring our hopes into reality.

The word 'birth' implies that this is our first time coming in, but on the contrary, it is more like the caterpillar being cocooned, and then the butterfly being birthed into the world. We have always been here, but being birthed through fire is a transformative process of going from who we have learned to be in a world that has shaped and scorned us into conformity. Transforming from the woman that has suffered, been hurt, fallen and got back up countless times. That felt She was never heard, seen or loved, at least not in the way She deserves. To the woman who has overcome, has been through adversity, heartache and pain. The woman who is READY to step up and become the Her that She deserves. This road is never easy, and it never will be, but being burnt and hurt in the past, in however many ways, you now emerge! Like a phoenix from the ashes, reclaiming your right to be here. Your right to take a stand, to be seen, heard and witnessed in all of your glory! Being birthed through fire and initiated into the flame. Being birthed into a new way of being.

Being birthed through fire is a RECLAMATION! An EXCLAMATION that you have well and truly ARRIVED!

She Who is Birthed Through Fire.

She who is birthed through fire.

The one whose power has been squashed, questioned, stomped on, deflated and cast aside, yet her embers remain burning deep.

Fuelled by the inner knowing that she IS more.

She came here to do, be, and thrive. But she bides her time, often unknowingly, jumping through the hoops of the trials and tribulations that each lifetime brings.

Meandering through Soul missions, each one adding to her infallible strength.

She may appear beaten, exhausted, at the end of her tether. Yet deep inside, a voice of sacred remembrance reminds her of her power, her strength, her higher mission.

She who is birthed through fire is humble yet powerful. Wounded with scars, she is still victorious. A symbolic image of her perilous journey to becoming who she is today.

Though others may cast their negativity, her inner flame is one that can never be extinguished, for the obstacles she faces serve as fuel to that fire.

To feed the flames of which she grows from, adding to her life force carried deep within.

She who is birthed through fire knows no bounds, though she has experienced them. They serve as walls to be shattered and cages to be freed from.

She who is birthed through fire is a gift onto this world. For she is part of the collective that will drive us forward into a new way of being. To create the change, to break the cycles, to stand as a pillar for those who are yet to come.

She who is birthed through fire, steps through the flames, commanding control of her demons, burning away all that is not of her highest good, restoring balance and harmony, wholeness and divine unity. Purposefully stepping into and embracing who she is at her core.

She who is birthed through fire forgives herself and releases and relinquishes fear, guilt, hurt or self-imposed pressure.

For she who is birthed through fire knows that, while we are powerful beings, we are in this human existence. To grow we must learn, yet to learn we must make mistakes. To free ourselves from mistaken judgments is to free ourselves from our inner monologue of fear and worry.

We are the women birthed through fire. We recognise our power and step forward into the flame, receiving all she offers, and casting ourselves into a light of strength, power and courage. We are the women who rise from the ashes, emerging from the flames, no matter how fierce, no matter how much they try to char our spirits.

We command the flame as a power of our own, not an obstacle to be feared or avoided. Initiated in a deep reverence and remembrance of all of She that we have been, all of She that we are, and all of She that we will become.

Into the fires together we ignite!

Initiation of the Flame

Fire is a beautiful thing! It can gift us warmth, light, safety, means to cook, bring people together and much more, but it can also burn and reduce gigantic things to nothing. But that is where we use it to our benefit - burning the aspects of our life that we despise, that we are tired of, that hurt us, that hold us back or make us feel less than we truly are. Igniting and awakening that glow within, even from the smallest spark, into a raging fire within that is unstoppable and ready to set the world alight! Despite being a Virgo - Earth sign - I am a Sagittarius Moon and that's where the Fire element really resonates, deep within my emotional self. It always felt like a guide, and something deeply embedded within me.

During my visits to Glastonbury, a huge sense of awakening happens within me, more so than any I've had ever before. The first time I visited Her chapel, I connected with the energy of St Margaret so strongly, receiving potent wisdom and guidance. First being taken on a visual journey of St Margaret's, then intertwined with my own journey. I have received, and continue to receive, various information on my visits. But it was on one of my visits to Glastonbury in 2022, whilst running a retreat and holding space for other women, I received the most profound download of them all.

'Initiation of the Flame'

At first, I thought it was something I had to seek out, a ceremony to attend and be initiated into. On further research and connection, I came to find there was no such thing. This was something that I was being guided to do, an offering that I HAD to gift out into the world. It was an initiation of sorts that I was to curate and make known!

But this book itself does not provide an initiation, and in getting this far, if you've reached this point, wondering when you will get to the initiation stage where I will talk you through a spectacularly sacred ceremony, then I am very sorry to disappoint you. This book offers not a specific initiation, but serves as a potent reminder, a beckoning, and a remembering of who you already are, deep at your core, all that you have been through, in this lifetime and lifetimes before, through lineages and sacred connections. Initiations and experiences that have been and will be bestowed upon you in many forms.

If you began this book, unsure of who you were, or perhaps just unsure of your ability and experience to connect to otherworldly beings, energies and concepts, then I hope by now that you have realised and shown appreciation for yourself. That you are already doing it, you just needed someone to shine a light on it all, and then see that light cascading onwards, illuminating your path ahead. I hope you will walk more awakened, more sure of yourself, with a more open heart and mind, and with a hunger to delve deeper into your own story.

Initiation of the Flame is to show you, that despite your experiences, inner narrative, and external hurdles, whatever factors have kept you small, delayed, resistant, or anything else that has felt like a big tough "NO!", that you CAN and you SHOULD! You have the power to grasp your life with both hands, to look back on where you've been, and to make the decision of where you are going. It is not and will not be easy at all, but the challenges are what enhances our resilience, ready to tackle each level as we ascend higher and higher into awareness and higher consciousness.

Now the misconception is often that things will be fine and dandy from here on in, but let me tell you, for many, this is just the beginning! Expect to move forward into both your spiritual awakening and your self-discovery like a white-knuckle ride and clinging on for dear life. Experiencing highs and lows, but from the perspective of knowing more about the bigger picture. Sometimes a blessing, sometimes a curse - as I mentioned previously in the book. But what matters is that you move forward, despite what life throws at you, with grit and determination to stay true to you. Although at times you may feel like you or the world around you is crumbling, to maintain that strong sense of self, or to know that you have your spirit team - of guides, ancestors, deities, whoever you resonate with and want to call in. They are with you, you are never alone, even if it physically seems so.

From here on, I invite and implore you to begin, return to, or continue sacred personal practice - however that may look and resonate for you.

But either way, I invite you to **Create an Altar Space**…

First and foremost, to be able to dedicate time and energy to yourself, it's much easier to have a focal point - a space. It gives you a sense of something that's just for you, somewhere you can focus your energy and also to create somewhere sacred that will aid you in coming into regular practice.

The concept may seem a bit "woo" if you're new to this, but essentially, you're just creating a bit of space that feels special to you. You may already have an altar, and in that case, perhaps take this opportunity to have a refresh, or just deepen your connection with it. If you don't have one already, then that's okay - this is your opportunity.

It can be as simple or as elaborate as you like. What matters most is that it feels special to you. It can be even as simple as some items on your bedside table or on a shelf. Place objects that are either meaningful to you, hold a positive energy or one that represents your intentions.

For example: -

- You may like to lay some fabric down.
- Add a candle (Obviously take fire precautions)

- Decorate with flowers, crystals, jewellery, figurines or any imagery that resonates.

You choose what goes on there. Although I guide you to not over complicate. If you are unsure, then leave it off. Only put items on there that feel good to you. It's not about how much stuff you can fit on, but how it makes you feel. If you want it to be as simple as a flower/petal and a tealight, that's fine!

This should feel like a dedicated space that you'd be happy to work with in sacred practice each day. This should stand you in good stead to establish a daily/regular practice of devotion and conscious time for yourself.

Connect in with and activate your altar. Perhaps light a candle, or do something that brings you into the space and signifies that you are open to work with it. Set your intention to deepen in, either in silence or if you want to play some music. And just sit. Just be. Hold your own space. Be conscious of your breath, focusing on the inhale and the exhale. Let your mind wander, indulge yourself. But don't let it wander into your to-do list, or anything you've been stressing over. Let it wander in a way that feeds your mind, your curiosity, that fills you with joy and expansion. Really revel in purposeful time spent with you.

Journal Prompts: -

How did you feel taking time for you?

Did you feel a sense of resistance or relief?

Did any specific thoughts, feelings or emotions come up?

She Is Here

As She reached through the trees, shifting the branches…

Glimmers of sunlight passed through, illuminating Her face, Her skin, shedding light on Her being here, in this moment.

In the golden rays of the sun, She takes a pause.

She has walked far, through many an obstacle, but She is here.

She is here, among the trees, the Earth, the Sun, the wildlife.

But She is also here among Herself - among Her innermost thoughts, Her desires, Her strengths, Her weaknesses. Her triumphs and failures.

She has journeyed far, yet still has far to go, but She is here.

She was bound, She was caged, She was kept small, Her divine light kept in the dark.

They told Her that She must, they told Her that She couldn't, they told Her that She would never be, they told her She was unworthy…

And for so long, She believed it.

She let the words and actions of ill intention anchor Her, trapped within an invisible cage of self-doubt, unworthiness and fear.

She was bound by guilt and shame that was instilled into Her by those who intended to weaken Her power, to dim Her essence and who feared what She was truly capable of.

She succumbed, enabling the words to penetrate Her being, to pierce Her spirit and wound Her heart.

But it was within this darkness, this pit of despair and woe, that Her inner flame flickered and grew brighter and brighter.

Nourishing Her from within, with the fire, strength and tenacity to become her own beacon of light and hope.

She became warm, radiant, and a beacon of inner hope for Herself and those around Her.

Her inner flame grew brighter and brighter. She became devoted to listening and feeling into the call of Her inner flame and deepest light.

The flames slowly engulfed all that had hurt Her, that had kept Her small or made Her shrink in self-doubt and disbelief.

And from here She took the first step, with complete love and devotion to Herself and Her divine being.

She knew that She was here for more.

She was not what had been spoken of Her, or who She had come to believe.

She was powerful, capable, beautiful, wise, wonderful, strong, all of which we were told or believed that She could never be.

And so, She embarked on Her journey, into the initiation of the flame.

An ascension into living her birthright and claiming that inner power as Her own.

Recognising who She is and who She came here to be.

Leaning into what lights Her up, what fills Her heart with joy.

Magnetising Herself to Her true soul tribe.

Surrounding Herself with the people, the places and the experiences She was sent here to receive and embrace.

Connecting with Herself and the Elements around her as She was intended to do so.

Among the trees, grounded into the soil, the cool breeze upon Her skin, She knelt at the stream, cupping the fresh water, splashing Her face and drinking in all that She needed.

She is connected. She is here. She is free. She is unbroken. She is unbound. She is aligned. She is ignited.

That inner fire burns within us all. We are so capable of being in devotion to our own divine light.

But first we must turn inwards. Lean into the call of the flame and initiate Her with open hearts, minds, souls and arms. Her power is within us all.

She who is birthed through fire.
Initiated by the flame,
The keeper of creativity, passion and femininity.
Blessed by Goddess.

A new cycle is dawning, a birth of creation.
A realisation of purpose and sovereignty. She who is the keeper of the flame, She who is birthed through fire.
Guiding others into the sacred light of the fire and flame.
Burning brightly, igniting the essence within, to see true beauty, true joy, true potential.
Shining a light on who she really is,
Stripping back and shedding the layers of which she has accumulated. By fire, by flame.
She is here!

I genuinely hope that this book, through my own story and experience, has created a space where not only have you felt heard and seen too, but it has offered the opportunity to welcome you into a space of open thinking. To know and realise that YOU are so worthy and deserving of all you desire in life, regardless of anything that has happened before this very moment. To rest and stand strong in the knowing that you are magnificent, and a life of wonder awaits you. A life of alignment, excitement, blessings, awakenings and so much more.

Always remember how incredible you truly are.

From my heart to yours, with love, gratitude and many blessings. Thank you for your time, space and energy.

Epilogue

As I have moved through writing this book, and through my own personal journey, I realise more and more that the 'work' is never done. While we may be personally elevating and awakening, that doesn't always bring us into a necessarily blissful existence. I mentioned in the book that 'ignorance is bliss' - it's still so true. The more you come into alignment with your true self, the more you see the things, people and situations that are out of alignment, and this just becomes more and more apparent as we excel in our personal uplevelings. Which brings the hard part - being caught in that 'catch 22', between a rock and a hard place, where you may find it difficult to move forward, leaving behind what has ever had you anchored and held back for so long. Or perhaps in a place where the empath in you truly believes that you can 'save' those people and situations so that they may level up with you. The sad but true thing is, we cannot be everyone's saviour. No matter how much our egoic self may really want the people or situations to remain, if it's not in our highest alignment, it will fall away, one way or another.

As I mentioned in the chapter *You Can Lead A Horse to Water,* we can have the best of intentions, but it may never even make a difference. We can hope and pray that someone is either saveable, or that we are able to support them fully into coming into alignment with their true self. In some cases we may be able to support people to do that, but more often than not, the ones that we really want to help are the ones that just don't give a shit. They're not interested, or they protest that they are 'just fine' and that's okay. Maybe it's not their time. But then comes the hard part for us, as we detach from these people, on purpose or not; it happens at some point. Those who are in full love and support will grow with you, in their own time, in their own way, still being supportive. Though those who have a bitter heart and mind will forever stay in that place, plateauing in their own dismay. Feeling like a victim with the whole world against them, taking offence to minor inconveniences, or just wallowing in a pit of despair and regret. One of the biggest lessons learnt is that it does hurt like hell, but you do have to speak up, put yourself first and, if needed, move forward without the love and support of those who are not aligned with you.

But how do you know they're not in alignment with who you are and are becoming? Because when you do speak up and put boundaries in place, rather than being met with understanding, you are met with hostility and perhaps even rejection. Or you feel a sense of dread, fear or resentment towards them. Maybe you feel those emotions from them, directed toward you. Often, the relationship will become hard work, either having to force it, feeling depleted because of it, or you may already feel it dwindling without even wanting to salvage it. Or there may be a situation where you do grow apart, not on purpose. Or perhaps there is some significant event (often seemingly out of the blue) where all your shit is blown wide open - maybe confrontation, disagreements, a chance to see everything for what it really is. Here this can go one of two ways - you may find the resolution you had been craving and hoping for, or it cements the knowing that this is no longer a positive relationship for you and this is the universe giving you a 'get out'.

Over the years, I have shed many people and situations as I have meandered through my own journey of self-discovery, healing, awakening and generally experiencing life. Sadly, some friendships had come to an abrupt end, some dwindled and others have been painful learning curves.

I have been through all of the aforementioned here in this book, and then some. Much of what I have shared is a first for me, in terms of sharing publicly other than with those closest to me. It has been challenging to write about, not in a painful way, but to move through it from my current state of being, where I can reflect back on situations without a broken victim mentality - a fairly new concept for me. Which in turn, for me, has been a very healing process. To revisit some of the most difficult times in my life, but to see it through the lens of who I am today has metaphorically ripped the band-aid off, giving it air and real space to heal.

I've also found that in sharing my own story, I have seen a different perspective at some points, I have felt a sense of achievement and pride, as well as seeing the areas where I still need to focus on. This book has given me a real opportunity to see how far I have come, long term, and to reaffirm all of the hard work I have put in to building the life I now live. Proving to myself, and others, that I did not let life get the better of me, that I may have made some wrong choices, but essentially, everything I have done up until now has led me to be the person I am today.

With that, I can say I am at a point now, where I am happy and proud of who I am. I can say that I got here, to this point, by choosing me or by choosing the options that felt most aligned. By learning to nurture myself, by loving her, respecting her, and by doing all that I have spoken of in this book. But also by doing the shadow work, meeting her in the darkness, acknowledging her, then being the beacon of light. That doesn't discount or invalidate, but that says *"I see you!"* and bears a torch for my shadow self to move forward, to find healing and acceptance, at her own pace.

Which is why I have told my stories, to show you that here, where and who I am right now. I can say that I have crafted a life that I love and am proud of. I also acknowledge all that has not been so great, rather than sweeping it under the rug and pretending it doesn't exist, and that you too are so capable of doing the same!

By no means am I living a blissful, carefree life where all is fine and dandy. And, of course, I have hopes, dreams and goals for the future; a vision for me to grow into. But I am living a life aligned with who I am right now. One that still offers me the lessons I need to experience to keep moving forward, but also offers me the opportunities to become my future self. Though I am able to look back on reflection on all the goals I've had previously and to see with good, hard evidence that they have come to fruition and that I am capable of being the version of me that I strive for, so with that evidence I must continue moving forward, not holding back. Reaching to achieve my goals, putting in the real footwork and making the effort. Experiencing the difficult and learning how to navigate because if it was easy then it wouldn't be worth doing.

I have yet to experience and learn many more things, as well as unlearning what I thought I knew. Even during the course of this book, my opinions and experiences have shifted. I have grown so much already, but to keep going back and editing this book each time would mean that it would never get finished, but just be an evolving diary! Hence why I have gone back and added Mini Epilogues to each chapter.

If my childhood self could see me right now, I know she would be proud. Not just because of the material things I have, but for the beautiful family I have created. A wonderful partner, great friends, a happy home, and to know that I am living my childhood dream. I get to create art every day. I get to choose how my day goes. I get to be me without having to hide any parts of who I am. Every day I revel in the beauty of life, in gratitude for my family - my wonderful children, the beautiful place in which I live, the opportunities that come my way, and to have the confidence to stand tall (at 5ft 1") with who I have become, despite all odds. That I never let my past restrict me, that I was able to come back into a place of alignment and appreciation for myself, regardless of all the hurt and sadness. That I was finally able to see my worth, to find love for myself, and go on to lead a life I both desired and deserved.

Nobody else gets to choose but you!

So to all of the versions of me - the ones who were hurt, felt unloved, taken advantage of, torn down, beaten and abused. The version who thought that she had failed, so many times. I don't stand here on a pedestal, but in a place of pride to remind her that she CAN and she DID. She overcame, she healed, she learned, she loved, she experienced, she danced, laughed, smiled and grew to enjoy the wonders of life. And I want you to know that YOU can too!

You too may be birthed through fire. You may have a lifetime filled with hurt and difficult experiences, yet still become a beacon of light, for yourself and others around you, as that flame in your belly burns brightly, fuelled in the knowing that you are always enough, and so much more! That you have the right to life everyday as you want to. Regardless of where you are right now, there is always a way up and out.

The first step starts with you believing you can. Not in a 'if you dream it you can do it' kind of way, but in a 'so tired of the same shit over and over again, what have you got to lose?!' kind of way! I hope this book ignites a spark within, showing you what is possible, and leads you either on your first or next steps towards self-discovery, appreciation and alignment. Or otherwise serves as a marker for you to reevaluate your current situation, to observe how you respond to yourself, others and the world around you, pivoting you toward a direction where you can begin, or continue, living from a place of love, in devotion to yourself, honouring your wants, needs, and also your hopes and dreams. Not in a way where you disregard everyone and everything else, but in a way that collaborates a sense of wonder, joy and inspiration for you and those who cross your path - known or unknown. Shine your light outward, without agenda, or any desire to receive in lieu. Just shine, and the world will shine with you, spilling light into the cracks, illuminating and transmuting all that is less than wonderful, giving opportunity for recognition, healing and release.

Perhaps this book may serve as a benchmark for you to finally stand up and be counted in a way that really matters. Where you finally feel able to say yes, or no, to what you want. Not out of spite, jealousy, bitterness, defeat of fear - instead out of love, respect, confidence, clarity and a more awakened state of being.

There is a whole world out there waiting for you, and while it will continue to wait, what use is waiting if you are never going to take the leap or even tip-toe in?

Helpful Link page

If you've been affected by or would like support for any of the themes mentioned in this book....

(Note: - These are U.K. links. If you are in need, please either reach out, or search for the equivalent support in your country of residence)

Mind Mental Health Charity: - https://www.mind.org.uk/

National Association for People Abused in Childhood: - https://napac.org.uk/

Women's Aid: - https://www.womensaid.org.uk/

National Autistic Society: - https://www.autism.org.uk/

Fibromyalgia Action U.K.: - https://www.fmauk.org/

SSAFA (Soldiers', Sailors' & Airmen's Families Association): - https://www.ssafa.org.uk/

Soul Musings

Yoni Prayer

I am here, I am present,

She is here, She is present.

A life force within me,

A source of power, courage, creativity, sensuality

From this place, I trust my power. I birth wonder into the world.

I release and relinquish any shame, hurt or fear that was ever laid upon me,

To wrongly instil negativity within my womb space.

This resides here no more.

I connect my Yoni energy with my heart's energy.

Filling Her with love, joy, adoration and celebration.

For She is within me, She is me, I am Her.

I henceforth and honour my divine femininity and welcome blessings of abundance and alignment into my life, my energy and into my sacred space.

And so, it is!

One Day...

She says -

One day I will achieve my dreams,

One day things will change,

One day I will speak up,

One day I will love who I am,

One day I will enforce my boundaries,

One day I will become a version of myself that is worthy!

But today is one day!

Believe in yourself,

Know that you can, you will, and you should!

Stop waiting for perfect circumstance, or terms that are befitting.

Use what you have to begin to facilitate your plans, to carve your plan and drive forward on your journey.

If we wait for the perfect day, it may never come, and instead of taking action and living a fulfilled life, we will have spent it waiting on a day that may never come!

Our ancestors didn't shout just so we could whisper!

Whistles and Whispers

Her essence whistles through, like a howling wind…
Sometimes you may choose to hide away, tuck yourself in and take shelter until it passes by…

Or would you choose to stand, with the wind blowing through your hair, listening to and witnessing all the divine wisdom and nourishment that She has to share…

How often Her essence flows through, but for so long we didn't see or hear it, we weren't conscious of it, or we chose to close our ears and our minds to what she had to deliver.

She comes with gentle whispers of love, hope, inspiration, support.

Sometimes with powerful notions, upgrades and awakenings.

But when we choose not to listen, instead, we hear her screeching, howling, vocally clawing away at us.

And we feel threatened and turn away.

Or we become frustrated when we don't understand the why.

What if those misunderstood howls were the nuggets of wisdom, we've been hoping for…

The promise of a better tomorrow, a better today, a better now…

Telling us that we are worthy.

That we do deserve,

That we do have the courage.

Others may not hear Her whistling whispers, nor will they understand.

But that is because they have turned themselves off from their own Soul whisperings.

They've become detached or perhaps indifferent to their true Soul yearnings.

But that's okay. It is not our job to save them, or to make them understand their own.

It is our job to listen to our own whispers, to the essence of Her that blows through, in the hopes that someday we can truly listen, hear, embody and transform into the divine beings we have always meant to be.

To embrace all that we are and all that
we can become, and truly shine.

To shine our beautifully unique light,
that nobody else can shine for us.

—

You are one, you are whole. A divine union of self.

A reclamation of embodiment. She ebbs and flows, as do you.

Perfection is not the goal. It is unison and self-trust.

The ability to speak your truth, regardless of who wants to hear it.

The ability to present as you are, exuding your true essence, regardless of who sees it.

The ability to discern, to make judgement on you and you alone, regardless of who speaks it.

Carry yourself forward and, in wholeness, in love.

Treat her unconditionally. Speak love, kindness, and empowerment into Her.
Nourish Her body, mind and spirit. Gift this glorious vessel the joy she craves.

Cradle Her and hold safe space for Her sadness and grief.

Celebrate Her and hold safe space for Her joy and accomplishments.

Nurture her and hold space for Her mistakes and explorations.

You need not external validation as proof of who and what you are. Be at peace and love with yourself. The world will follow.

—

Welcome home to the parts of you that have long been lost or forgotten.

Welcome home to the Soul fragments since restored.

Welcome home to the fiery essence within, of the woman who has awakened and is ready to rise.

For she was never incomplete, just rested. entwined in a deep forgetting.

But she is restored, with a resounding cheer, filled with love and happiness.

Welcome home to the woman who has realised her strength and remembered who she is.

Welcome home to the divine union of herself, the light & dark, yin & yang, Shakti & Shiva, the feminine & masculine.

For she who sees through balanced eyes will discover and explore the true universe of infinite possibility, abundance, and opportunity that lays before her.

Welcome home, sister. Welcome home!

Surrounded by the walls built to keep us small, contained and complacent.

A flicker of hope, a dream, a wish, manifests into motivation and determination.

We begin to unspeak the words and derobe the opinions cast

upon us. Shedding the skins acquired by those with intention to break us. Releasing all that has caged, diluted and silenced who and what we truly are.

We discover, nurture and embrace the woman within, releasing a primal roar, a resounding scream, to reclaim us, our freedom, who we are, who we came here to be.

We break down those walls and break the chains, freeing ourselves, stepping into our divinity, to reclaim and live the life of joy that you so rightly deserve.

—

Stay A While

Stay a little while, she said…

Take some time to recharge, relax, and rest your head.

Your eyes have been fuzzy, your head a little dizzy, your hands on the go, your body's been busy.

So stay a while, lay yourself down and take what you need.

The world will not cease.

Then the guilt sets in, and there's stuff to be done, but stay a little while, you're priority number one.

Stay a little while, take sanctuary and space.

Know that this time is yours, your sacred place.

Revel in the time, it's yours to keep.

Find quiet, find stillness, not a sound, not a peep.

Or make some noise, dance, scream and shout,

For this time is yours, express yourself, have no doubt.

But stay a little while,

Take it slow, or raise the bar.

Reset, or rejoice, meet yourself wherever you are.

Initiation of the Flame

By heart, by womb, you are connected as one.

By yoni, by essence, you are rebirthed.

As you are held within the circle of light and portal of fire,

You are seen, you are witnessed.

As your inner embers spark and ignite, your fire within burns brightly.

She is awakened.

You are blessed,

As you are birthed through fire and initiated by the flame.

She Knew

She was held,

She was cleansed,

She released.

She relaxed,

She knew.

She knew she was held,

She knew she was cleansed,

She knew she was released,

She knew she was relaxed,

She trusted in gifting herself time and space - to heal, to be.

She was reminded of all of the things she knew when she gifted herself time and space.

I am good enough just as I am.

I am loved by those who are meant to love me.

I am responsible for my own joy and happiness.

I am not bound by generational patterns.

I have the power to create and come home to my own destiny.

I live regardless of judgment.

I am valid.

I am seen as I need to be.

I do not need approval, for it is already there within.

I do what I love because I love it.

I know that aligned abundance will come without having to burn myself out.

I am here living and fulfilling my soul mission.

I am in too deep to be distracted by anything that could undo my purposeful doing.

The Altar

The altar burns brightly.

A space of love and devotion.

To gift our offering and to replenish our Souls.

Honour thy Altar, the space for your Soul devotion and dedication.

A space where she may come alive, be healed, inspired, held, and loved.

Open your heart to sacred practice.

Open to devotion.

Gift the love and attention you wish to receive.

The need to be found, heard and acknowledged.

Inner child crying out for help.

She is seen,

She is heard,

She has the ability and power to find herself.

You no longer need to cry out to be found.

You know the way.

Remember why you are here and who you came here to be.

She who is birthed through fire,

Reborn from the ashes of hurt, trauma, and suppression.

Here to reclaim and reignite the flame of your own and those who choose you for guidance.

You are fire!

Burn all that does not grace you and use the flame to illuminate your path forward.

Never forget who you are.

She whispers gently,

The words echo deeply through her being.

Her essence, touching her soul,

bringing her to remembrance, unity and wholeness.

The words she whispers -

Like a flame, burn brightly, take your place, illuminate, feel the heat rise within,

for the fire burns endlessly from within a woman in true embodiment of her joy, her truest form.

Releasing and relinquishing pain and hurt and beaming like a pillar of light,

standing in her power, proclaiming to the world "*I am here!*",

and shining as a beacon of hope to themselves,

inspiring, and giving unconditional love and space.

For she who is in tune with her inner fire and true essence will break the mold and pave the way for the women and men that come after us.

Contributing to creating and welcoming true harmony and universal love back to our Mother Earth.

Guidance Readings

Reading One

Set your intention, take a deep breath and choose a number from below, then turn the page to reveal your reading

| One | Two | Three |

ONE

You have more within you than you know. You are embracing what is within and already rising up. Now you must trust that you hold enough skill and wisdom to share with others. Others will trust in you and you mustn't be afraid to let them. Know that you are capable. Self-belief will take you a long way!

TWO

If you are contemplating something in your life, take this as confirmation that you can do it and you should. You are likely a careful thinker, and will often meticulously choose and plan, however in this instance, you have been in two minds and your heart and heart have been telling you different things. Go for it, say yes! It seems you have exhausted all angles of *what if,* so allow yourself to surrender to your heart, trust your intuition and go forth and do it!

THREE

There's a gut feeling you have and you're not sure if it's just fear or if it's worth paying attention to. Trust the niggle, you are more than likely right. Go with your instincts and don't allow yourself to fall into any traps of negativity. You can carry your own, so don't be fearful of losing any "safety nets". Perhaps cutting loose is the opportunity you need to see that you can truly fly in what you aim to do.

Reading Two

Set your intention, take a deep breath and choose a number from below, then turn the page to reveal your reading

One *Two* *Three*

ONE

You are more supported than you think. The divine are sending you messages of guidance and hope. You have a strong linage and have strong spiritual connections, be it in this life or your past lives. You are never alone, so when in need, do not hesitate to call upon your own council of light. Allow yourself to feel held and guided without hesitation or second guessing. Just as others have shone a light before you, you are your own beacon of light, spreading love and joy into the world. You are protected, so go forth without fear.

TWO

You are stronger than you think, however it appears you may be stalling or putting something off. Have faith and confidence in yourself! There is so much out there waiting for you, but you need to step forward to receive it. Amazing things are unfolding for you and you have so much opportunity to grow. However, you must be strong enough to grab it with both hands and own it as your own. It is your time to be amazing in your own right! You have likely been in the background of someone else's plans and progress, but you are incredible too. Warrior woman appears here to give you the strength you need to step forward and follow your path with confidence.

THREE

You hold so much within, it must be shared with others. You will gain more knowledge by sharing your own wisdom. It is time now to take things up a level and recognise that you are more than ordinary, more than simple, more than plain. You hold so much power within, though you may not even know it. Trust in yourself and believe, then others will follow. Now is a time to pass on knowledge or guidance to those who need it and will trust in your words and actions. Others love and adore you more than you realise. Also remember to love yourself, to see the good that is within and to honour yourself as the incredible being that you are.

Reading Three

Set your intention, take a deep breath and choose a number from below, then turn the page to reveal your reading

One   *Two*   *Three*

ONE

You may be feeling overwhelmed right now at future prospects or hope that you have for the future. However, being sure that this is what you want will help you massively this week. Don't be overwhelmed by it all as you are more than capable, just take things at your own pace before diving right in headfirst. There will likely be obstacles, but pre-empting now and doing careful planning will help you to avoid the bulk of any troubles along the way. Be prepared. Failing to prepare is preparing to fail!

TWO

Why so tense? Don't be afraid to show your true self and your true feelings. Something has got your back up recently and you may be feeling defensive or that someone has got it in for you. However, you have more power than you realise. Don't allow others' negativity to capture you. You are strong and fantastically independent. Lay down your metaphorical sword and, instead of wasting energy fending off negativity, use your energy to create and welcome more positivity into your life.

THREE

Changes are afoot for you and you may be in a phase where you feel a shift but don't know how or why. Know that anything occurring right now is to carry you forward into the next phase of your life. Embrace the opportunities given to you and try not to second guess too much. You are becoming more enlightened and are set for true growth. Too much time overthinking will leave you underwhelmed with your choices and decisions. Believe in yourself and know that you can do more than you give yourself credit for. The next step in your journey is trusting and believing in yourself!

Reading Four

Set your intention, take a deep breath and choose a number from below, then turn the page to reveal your reading

One *Two* *Three*

ONE

Take this time to gather your thoughts and take cover before jumping into something right now. You may feel like you have the answer or solution, but just take a little extra time to sit on it before taking action. You will find that in doing so, more useful information or opportunities will come to light to give you more success in what you are endeavouring to do.

Also at this point, any offers that come your way from something very much "off plan", may seem enticing, but do not feel like you need to say yes. This will most likely lead you astray and take you back to square one. Stick to your own plan and don't jump into anything too soon without proper thought.

TWO

At this point in time you may be feeling like you want to withdraw yourself and spend more time in your own thoughts. That is not a bad thing. Think of it as stepping back from the hustle and bustle of conscious life and allowing your subconscious to receive and download higher information, which can then be transferred to your conscious mind. Being alone isn't a bad thing, as actually you're never really alone, the energies around you will use this time to communicate and give you what you need. Never feel guilty for wanting some alone time.

THREE

You have everything you need, so why are you waiting? What's putting you off? Do not fear taking the first step, or making a move. Take it all in your stride, for now is the time. You may be afraid of things going wrong, but if you don't try it, then you will never know. Take that first step and you will feel the rest follow naturally. If you're still feeling uneasy about moving forward, take some time to reflect on your progress so far. Use your experiences as a drive to take you forward. Good things are waiting for you, and you know this. Now it's your time to leap and grasp them.

Reading Five

Set your intention, take a deep breath and choose a number from below, then turn the page to reveal your reading

One *Two* *Three*

ONE

Things are falling into place. You are harnessing more personal power, and becoming more aware of who you truly are and can be. Now you must realise how incredible you are and allow your light to shine brighter than it ever has before. Take time to breathe and go deep within, to connect with your soul, and consciously hear the words "it is now safe to flourish".

TWO

You are being reminded that you are not here for a sole purpose, but a divine purpose and duty to yourself and the Divine. This is your calling, to step up and begin to share your knowledge, skill and talent, while also carrying it out. You have learnt, and now you should raise your energetic vibration by passing down your knowledge. Your purpose here is greater than the mundane, and you must believe that you are here for more than just the daily grind. Relinquish any fear, for you were always meant for more!

THREE

A deepened connection with your past lives is calling you here. You must go back in order to move forward. In this lifetime you are being summoned to recollect, acknowledge and implement your past life learnings. Your soul has been on an epic journey of specific purpose and in this instance you must adapt your current living life to accommodate this. To do so, you must become more aware of your prior skills, knowledge, experiences and perhaps even sufferings from previous lifetimes and existences. Realise how you can use those lessons to expand in this lifetime and to continue the legacy of seriously deep soul work which your higher self has been working on for quite some time.

Reading Six

Set your intention, take a deep breath and choose a number from below, then turn the page to reveal your reading

One *Two* *Three*

ONE

There is more to you than meets the eye and it's about time you shared that with others. Embrace who you truly are and put yourself out there to provide support and solace for others through your own life lessons. You may be surprised at what another person admires about you, but this is because we rarely recognise our own strengths.

TWO

The only person holding you back right now is yourself. There is much waiting for you but for some reason you are resisting. Perhaps a lack of confidence or fear of failure? You have everything you need and more to make progress and achieve results. Believe in yourself and take the next step. You will thank yourself. Better a whoops, than a what if!

THREE

Your surroundings have a big influence on you right now, so be sure that you are immersing yourself in the right kind of places. Perhaps a change of scenery will do you good too, but pay extra attention to your regular surroundings and make any amendments required. The energy and aesthetic around the body can have a strong impact inside the body and mind. It is important to keep this in mind.

Reading Seven

Set your intention, take a deep breath and choose a number from below, then turn the page to reveal your reading

One   *Two*   *Three*

ONE

What is your true direction right now? Come back to you, your authentic self, and ask yourself what lights you up? What truly calls to you, regardless of outer judgement, pressures or any other external influences? Go deep within to find and discover what makes your soul sing. What intrigues you? What do you want to know more about? What do you want to do more of? At this moment in time, you may find you are questioning yourself and your direction, but also perhaps feeling a bit lost within space and time. That's because you need to find yourself again. Find you and be the most you that you've ever been. Your soul is craving to lead its true, authentic path. Don't be afraid of others, for they are not on this journey. Be incredibly you and the people that matter will still be on this incredible journey with you. Your path awaits, you just need to fully discover it first before taking the first step.

TWO

This choice gives off the energy similar to that of a butterfly emerging from the chrysalis. You have undergone big changes, or perhaps been shut off from a world you were once familiar with or felt comfortable in, but now this is the time that things step up. You are not the same person you used to be, but do not approach that with sadness or grief. There is no need to mourn the old you. For you are still you, but a more elevated, empowered and knowledgeable you.

Changes around you are not happening to cause you pain. They are happening to make way for the next step of the journey, which will give you the correct tools to progress in your soul's journey. Welcome in change, whether it be looked at with a negative gaze. Make it work for you. The universe is sending you this for a special reason. Do not feel beaten or lost. Own it and embrace it and use these coming changes to grow into the amazing being you are.

THREE

You are becoming part of your soul tribe. You are connecting with the people and the energies that will support you in your journey, your growth and your soul's true calling.

In choosing this option, it asks you to become more aware of your current energetic state, and to really honour who you are right now. You possess such wonderful gifts, such special knowledge, and you can both learn and teach at this point. As children of the universe, we will forever learn, but there comes a point when we are able to share our knowledge with others, be it on a professional level, or a personal level. Now is the time to honour everything that you are and to embrace the true strength of what you hold within.

Reading Eight

Set your intention, take a deep breath and choose a number from below, then turn the page to reveal your reading

One   *Two*   *Three*

ONE

Let down your barriers and try to not be so serious all the time, you do not need to be the one always in control, or the one that has to mediate everything. It may feel like "*If I don't, then who will?*" but in doing so, this gives those around you the opportunity to step up and do their bit, perhaps mature, or take on more responsibility, while also giving you time to do more of the fun things and to not feel like the weight and stress is all on you. Release full control, stress and the feeling of having to be in charge all of the time!

TWO

It may seem like you are really striving for an answer, when perhaps you are doing it already, or maybe you know what to do, but you just aren't doing it yet. To come into alignment, the Universe is asking you to trust. Trust yourself and what you are feeling and step fully into doing the thing. Reassess and see what isn't working for you, and in letting go of that, it will bring you closer to alignment.

THREE

You are being called to release old patterns of a life that you have always known has never fitted you. You are being called back to the old ways, but to do so, you must release from the binds of modern conformity, the need to "fit" and also the need to please. The Universe asks that you release old thought processes that are holding you back, to release any negative beliefs about yourself or your life path and know that a new life path is there. Know that you cannot walk it if you are still attuned to old habits or beliefs that are hardwired in from the current or previous path that was not aligned for you.

Reading Nine

Set your intention, take a deep breath and choose a number from below, then turn the page to reveal your reading

One *Two* *Three*

ONE

You must step out of old patterns, either your own, ancestral, or past life. These are patterns that have recurred to either give a lesson, or experience so that change can occur. This card invites you to be that change, to recognise the pattern and to say *"No, this ends with me!"*. For you are not only doing this for yourself, but for your lineage. So, this will impact you now, but also further down your path when you have created that open pathway for them. To align here, there is healing, discovery and changes to be made. It won't be easy, for if it was, the chain would have been broken by now, but you are here now in this opportunity to do it, to be the one, so trust that you are capable and worthy of not only breaking away from what has held you and others back for so long, but you have the opportunity to be truly free and happy.

TWO

Release those around you that do not respect your boundaries, the people that push and push, yet never learn. You are not here to save them, nor to make them understand. Enforcing clear boundaries will help both you and them on your paths. This also asks you to release the need to save everyone, to be the hero and the fixer. By all means do help where you'd like to, but this calls to reinforce that you are not here to fix and appease those that are not necessarily willing to do the work for themselves. Release the feeling of having to be the people pleaser, or to shrink yourself to make others comfortable. Find your voice and set those boundaries!

THREE

To bring yourself into alignment, you must nurture yourself and be the caregiver, but to yourself. Give yourself not just the necessities of what you need, but also give yourself the love, softness and nurturing that a mother would to their own child. To bring yourself into alignment, recognise that you are worthy of love and gentleness, of being seen, heard and appreciated. That it is not bad to give that to yourself. This card may also ask you to look into any mother wounds you may have and perhaps dedicate some time and space to giving yourself either what you never had, what you needed more of, or maybe just reminding yourself that you are worthy of love and care too.

Printed in Great Britain
by Amazon